HOW TO BE RICH: THE SECRET AGENT METHOD:

BY COLIN NICHOLAS

COPYRIGHT NOTICE

ACKNOWLEDGEMENT AND THANKS

I would like to thank everyone who helped me put this book together. Special thanks go to Andy Bounds (author of *The Jelly Effect: How to Make Your Communication Stick*), Ben Kench (author of *Selling for Dummies*), and Arvind Devalia (author of *Make it Happen for Yourself and the World,*

PRAISE FOR HOW TO BE RICH: THE SECRET AGENT METHOD

This powerful book gives you proven tools you can use to sell more, faster and easier, in any market.

~Brian Tracy, bestselling author, The Way to Wealth *and* Eat That Frog!

This is an intelligent and well-crafted book, which applies well-founded psychological principles to the persuasion process. I recommend it.

~Dr. Robert Levine, PhD, professor of Psychology at California State University, bestselling author of The Power of Persuasion: How We're Bought and Sold.

This book is chock-full of useful strategies to give you the spark you need to be wealthy. Colin wants you to be rich. Give him a chance to help you get there!

~Kevin Hogan, bestselling author of The Science of Influence *and* Covert Persuasion. *Kevin has worked as*

an expert advisor on persuasion and influencing for ABC, Fox, the BBC, The New York Times, New York Post, Forbes, Investor's Business Daily, *and* Cosmopolitan.

This inspiring and challenging book will make you jump out of your comfort zone while at the same time entertaining you. This is one book which is sure to kick-start your life and to help you to take it a few levels higher up from wherever you are now. Read this book, leave behind your presumptions about how great life can be, and you will be pleasantly surprised how quickly and dramatically your life is transformed!

~Arvind Devalia, bestselling author of Make It Happen for Yourself and the World.

There is no doubt about it. If you are serious about success and making your life better, the wisdom contained within this book will be invaluable when you learn it, absorb it, and apply it. An excellent success tool for your toolbox!

~Ben Kench, www.thebusinessbooster.co.uk

I really enjoyed this book. I like the emphasis on practical advice. I regularly work with moving my clients in the same direction. I found this book to be very direct, supportive, and challenging and, at the same time, consistently focused on helping the reader.

~Mike Bryant, consultant, hypnotherapist and author of Self-Hypnosis for Dummies.

Some great ideas to help you convince more people more often ... and more pleasantly for both you and them!

~Andy Bounds, UK Sales Trainer of the Year and bestselling author of The Jelly Effect: How to Make Your Communication Stick

I found this book very interesting; my only concern is that it might find its way into the hands of nefarious individuals!

~Rory Sutherland, vice chairman of Ogilvy & Mather Group UK and columnist at The Spectator magazine (Britain's oldest magazine)

TABLE OF CONTENTS

EXTENDING THE HAND OF FRIENDSHIP

FOREWORD

If you want to embark on an exciting adventure of fortune, freedom and fun, then you have certainly come to the right place. A life of pink diamonds, Fabergé eggs, Château Lafite champagne, and Lamborghini Reventons really is within your grasp if you so desire it.

It's fair to say that Colin is a true genius. Over the years I have read literally dozens of self-help books, and this is a different kettle of fish altogether. A lot of literature in this genre is seemingly written from a sort of New Agey, nonscientific point of view. Those authors are far more concerned with telling the reader that they need to think about things from a new perspective than explaining *how* to actually go about doing that with hard facts. This is what separates Colin's seminal work from the competition.

Also, to be completely honest, most self-help books have their heads way too far up their own backsides, while Colin often has his tongue firmly in cheek, which is very refreshing too. As Oscar Wilde famously said, "Life is far too important to be taken seriously."

I read Colin's book when I was experiencing a very dark period in my life. My real estate business was rapidly going down the tube, and I owed a veritable fortune to various unpleasant creditors. I was inundated with nasty visits and threatening phone calls from debt collectors on a daily basis. The vultures were circling malevolently, and the wolf was waiting menacingly at the door. I was just about reaching the end of my tether as I wondered how I could put food on the table.

My financial fortunes underwent a surprising but very welcome volte-face when a high-flying acquaintance of mine recommended to me Colin's book. Initially I was naturally skeptical, but I thought, *Hell, I have nothing to lose. I might as well give it a shot.* The rest, as they say, is history!

Now, at a tender young age, I am delighted to admit that I have amassed sufficient wealth to retire in considerable comfort. My biggest worry in life is pondering which exotic cocktails to quaff with lunch and which five-star hotel to visit for my next outrageously luxurious vacation.

None of us are here forever, and life is short. So read this book, follow the instructions and enjoy the ride!

Ruihua Li, Beijing- market leading retail entrepreneur and winner of the Herrick Business Award 2014 for the most innovative start-up

INTRODUCTION

So who the hell is Colin Nicholas? Let me tell you a little bit about myself. I had a very standard type of upbringing. I grew up in a small market town in England in the 1980s and 1990s. I was educated at the local state school. My parents were regular middle-class professionals. We weren't poor, but we were not rich by any means. Overall my background was very commonplace and ordinary.

Upon leaving school, I scraped by admittance into a well-respected university; it ranked in the UK's top ten at the time. Regrettably I was too hotheaded for college at that age and was forced to leave without graduating after several unfortunate incidents, which I would prefer not to elaborate upon. Fortunately another university (not quite as prestigious but still decent enough) agreed to take me in. I managed to leave with a reasonable degree—my parents breathed a sigh of relief!

I spent several glorious months searching for a graduate job, interspersed with some halfhearted casual work and a healthy dollop of idle philandering. Then, much to everyone's surprise, I secured a place on a highly regarded graduate trainee program. Bursting with enthusiasm (sort of!), I packed my bags and cheerfully set off for London. I stayed on the same career path for about ten years, drifting around the organization and somehow getting a couple promotions.

I wasn't *unhappy* with my life over the next few years. My job could have been (slightly) worse. I made a few really great buddies at work, and this allowed me to punctuate the long periods of corporate monotony with some rather fun-filled times. Nevertheless, as time passed, my contentment slowly began to evaporate into thin air. I was actually doing quite well for myself, especially compared to many of my old school chums. However, I became increasingly aware that my pay paled in comparison to some of the real high rollers in London. This made me increasingly dissatisfied with my own position in life and my financial circumstances. For instance:

- Rather than residing in a smart abode in an exclusive location, I lived in a modest house in an average neighborhood. I invariably felt guilty when I implied to people that I lived somewhere classier or even told outright lies about the issue. The problem is that people often make irreversible judgments about you based upon superficial things, like where you live.

- Instead of the high-performance sports cars that wealthy people favor, I drove a run-of-the-mill secondhand car. I always pretended not to notice when someone cruised arrogantly past me in a fashionable luxury vehicle or disdainfully cut me off. However, I felt rather resentful inside, especially since I worked so damn hard and still couldn't afford something like that.

- Dressing smartly was a vital part of my job, but I was chronically short of money. So, instead of visiting a first-class tailor and ordering a high-quality garment, to fit my particular physical requirements, I made do with an off-the-rack suit from a standard main-street chain. When meeting important people, I couldn't help but feel somewhat self-conscious about the fact that they were much better dressed than me.

- I desperately wanted to donate to several worthwhile charities, such as BBC Children in Need, Oxfam, and so on, but I could never afford to provide a substantial donation or set up a regular direct debit.

- Despite earning reasonable money, I always seemed to struggle with my finances. The cost of living appeared to get higher and higher, and I was always unpleasantly surprised by how little was left in my bank account at the end of the month.

- I occasionally browsed celebrity magazines, even though I am generally uninterested in gossip or trivia. I felt anger bubbling up inside me when I considered how moronic celebrities could buy anything they wanted without making any real effort in life. Conversely ordinary people are compelled to work like slaves just to get by, feed their kids, and have a roof over their heads.

- I could never afford to take my kids to the sort of stylish holiday resorts which my friends' families visited. Instead I was always forced to settle for cheap package deals. I didn't mind that much personally, but my wife and children always looked sad and forlorn when I told them that we couldn't afford to go to nicer (and more expensive) places.

- My wife loves designer Italian shoes. They are her passion and the only thing she will waste money on! However, I could only afford to get her standard shoes from an ordinary main-street shop for Christmas. She never complained, but I would love to have bought her a pair from her favorite designer.

I know this sounds rather petty and materialistic. I later realized that there is much more to life than material possessions. I should also add that I am not looking for sympathy or complaining in any way. I am fully aware that the vast majority of people in the world are in much worse financial situations than me, but I desperately didn't want to settle for a normal life. I was utterly sick and tired of just "getting by" and "keeping my head above water." In my heart I secretly knew I wanted more much than that. I wanted to experience the full trappings of the celebrity lifestyle.

I constantly pondered the question of why only a tiny proportion of people live the high life, while the rest settle for second best. This question began to totally obsess me. I frenziedly searched everywhere for the answer to this conundrum. I vociferously read the biographies of famous political leaders, like Theodore Roosevelt, Winston Churchill and Napoleon, plus business tycoons, such as George Soros and Donald Trump.

My research gradually led me to the sad understanding *that I just didn't have the personality required to achieve greatness*. I compared myself to famous figures in history and regretfully concluded that, while they had personalities of solid steel, mine was more like cheap plywood. Let me give you just a few examples:

- I had dreams; I had desires, and I had aspirations, but I generally didn't follow my heart. This is because I was unbearably scared of the consequences of failure. I was like a horse that went up to the water but was afraid to jump. For instance, I realized that I was wasting my time in my current job, but I just didn't have the bravery required to quit and strike out on my own.

- My attitudes toward relationships had similar shortcomings. I was infatuated with this beautiful woman I knew. I dreamed about her constantly, but, to my frustration, it took me years to muster up sufficient nerve to ask her out on a date (I eventually married her, but I wasted years procrastinating).

- I spent hours and hours worrying about the future, especially about my family's financial security. I wondered what would happen to us if I lost my job. How would I pay the bills? Would I be a tremendous disappointment to my wife? Who would support my beloved children? Would they have to attend a bad school in a dodgy neighborhood? I realized full well that this incessant worrying was completely unproductive, but, in spite of myself, I just couldn't help doing it.

- I was sometimes confident and extroverted. For example, when socializing with my teammates at work, who I knew well, I was quite outgoing. Indeed, at times, people actually saw me as "the life and soul of the party." But often, such as when dealing with important people, I felt utterly insecure. My confidence simply evaporated when I was in the presence of very senior people, such as our company's impressive new CEO. When speaking to this sort of person, I felt shamefully inferior and on edge.

- I attempted to project an independent and self-contained demeanor to others. However, I was intensely preoccupied with what other people thought of me, especially whether or not they liked me. If I did find out that someone disliked me, then it upset me terribly for days. As a consequence I often did things just to please others, even when I knew that it wasn't the right thing to do. For instance, I spent a huge amount of time at work, performing useless tasks just to keep my idiotic boss happy. I secretly hated dancing to other people's tunes, but nevertheless I still did it.

- I found it difficult to take the bull by the horns and tackle challenging issues head-on. I realized, on an intellectual level, that being successful often requires making tough decisions. However, whenever possible, I shied away from making hard choices.

- When I actually forced myself to make a difficult call, I worried relentlessly about whether or not I had done the right thing. I felt extremely guilty and continuously turned the problem over and over in my mind. This just wasted my time and got me nowhere in terms of solving the issue. I hated being so pathetically weak-minded, but I just couldn't help it.

- I was desperate to make a positive impact at work but found doing so a real struggle. I am actually quite a creative person. I had an abundance of great ideas about how to make our company more profitable. If only my foolish boss would have listened, my suggestions could have generated a fortune in extra profits! To my incredible frustration, he generally dismissed my brilliant proposals out of hand.

- I experienced similar problems in climbing the slippery career ladder. I got stuck in one particular dead-end job for several monotonous years. Exasperatingly I knew I possessed the ability to progress further, yet, for some reason, I always fluffed the job interviews. I found it very tricky to create the right impression. I hated going home to tell my loyal wife that I had failed to get the job *again*.

As I became ever more conscious of my blatant shortcomings, I started getting rather dispirited. As time passed, I became progressively more disheartened. I felt persistently stressed, lethargic, and bored. My interest in both work and socializing began to wane. I spent more and more time alone at home, mindlessly watching television and aimlessly moping around. I found sleep elusive, tossing and turning in bed until the early hours of the morning. This left me feeling exhausted throughout the daytime. To compound my problems, I drank to increasing excess. Eventually I was habitually knocking back about eight cans of strong lager every night. I became tired and irritable. I piled on the pounds, which further still knocked down my self-esteem.

Initially my wife, friends, and family were incredibly supportive, but, as my malaise dragged on and on, their sympathies gradually ran short. My wife eventually started dropping hints that she and the children might leave me. These hints finally became explicit threats. This deterioration in my marriage came as a tremendous shock to me, because it was a reminder of how far I had sunk. My situation became so heartbreaking that I wondered whether life was even worth living.

However, just as my situation worsened to an intolerable level of psychological suffering, a dramatic upturn in my circumstances transformed my life forever. A strange series of events led to me being offered a bizarre opportunity, in which I learned the hidden secrets of wealth generation. As I systematically applied these secrets, I was taken aback when I observed how rapidly I had accumulated more and more prosperity, achievements, freedom, and profound admiration from others.

Are you prepared to follow in my footsteps and embark on the path to unlimited fortune and adventure? Ask yourself the following simple questions to find out:

- Are you willing to spend a mere single day of your life reading this explosively potent book, which could potentially deliver you riches beyond your wildest fantasies? When pondering this question, consider that many people spend *four years or more* at university, studying a subject that often has little practical benefit once they enter the world of employment.

- Are you ambitious for the sort of financial accomplishment that will make your jealous acquaintances hate you? Do you want it *now*, rather than scrimping, saving, and making sacrifices until you reach old age to obtain your financial freedom?

- Do you want to achieve the real prosperity that you and your family truly deserve, instead of being laughed at by the arrogant superrich for leading a mediocre life?

If you answered yes to all these questions, then congratulations! You are fully prepared to commence your exhilarating voyage to greatness. If not, then I am afraid that this book isn't really for you. You just don't have the get-up-and-go required to make the grade. I sincerely apologize for wasting your time and bid you farewell.

So, for those who are still reading, let's commence our quest without further ado. The first part of your secret-agent training for success is to reverse the brainwashing which you have been subjected to all your life. This will help you uncover this book's *hidden secret message*.

CHAPTER ONE: THE DARKEST SECRETS OF THE SUPERRICH

Wealth is the product of man's capacity to think.

—Ayn Rand

A   I CAN HELP YOU ACHIEVE YOUR WILDEST DREAMS

Prepare to embark on the journey of a lifetime. In Chapter One, I will explain why it is so incredibly desirable to set sail to the opulent and exotic land of the superrich. I will also reveal why you need to drastically change course if you ever want to reach this enviable destination. You will hear the following:

- Success is simply a matter of copying other incredibly successful people (you should realize that it really is that straightforward)

- You are currently experiencing *The Matrix*—not true reality (unfortunately you have spent your whole life laboring under an illusion)

- Everything you have been taught about how to get rich is a complete lie (prepare to learn the shocking truth)

- To obtain true wealth you must channel the essence of a daring secret agent (this might sound strange, but all will be revealed)

I will tell you how to harness the spirit of an elite secret agent to hopefully acquire the sort of mind-boggling wealth that will make superstar celebrities jealous. The global superrich elite really don't want you to know this stuff.

There are so many books out there purporting to explain "the secrets of getting rich," and telling you how to make your fortune and so on, that it's rather tough to know who to believe. There are so many authors making ridiculous claims that it's insane.

However, if you dream of achieving abundant financial success and of having an enjoyable and exciting time doing so, then I believe this is the most important book you'll ever read.

Applied correctly, the secrets in this book will help you to escape the boredom, humiliation, and inconvenience of the daily grind, which is getting tougher and tougher because of recession and austerity.

You need not settle for the hard and mediocre life that 99 percent of people endure, which, due to global economic forces and trends, is only likely to get even more dismal. The good news is that you can learn to escape from the hardship and struggles of ordinary life, such as:

- Scrimping, saving, and worrying about money; fretting over whether you can afford to pay the bills, to purchase the home or car you really deserve, to build up a reasonable pension, to provide your children with a high-quality education, or to meet the expenses of decent healthcare for yourself, your partner, or your parents in their old age.

- *Instead you can obtain all the wealth that you and your loved ones require to enjoy a happy and prosperous life. You can accumulate this opulence at warp speed. Not only that but you can also enjoy an adventurous, fun, and exhilarating time amassing your fortune.*

- Bitterly regretting wasting your precious life doing a mind-numbing and monotonous job, while answering to the beck and call of a tedious and ignorant boss, for a meager paycheck.

- *Rather it is possible to quickly become so astoundingly loaded that the stresses and tensions of the rat race will become a distant memory. This allows you to immediately begin spending your time meaningfully and productively on activities of your own choosing. These could include social, spiritual, or family-related pursuits.*

So how can I help you to accomplish this dramatic transformation in your financial fortunes? It's stunningly straightforward. My simple and humble suggestion is that becoming a full-fledged member of the global elite is simply a matter of accurately replicating both the *mind-set* (which I call the "inner game") and the *capabilities* (the "outer game") that the 0.001 percent invariably possesses.

Why do some individuals become multimillionaires and billionaires, while the overwhelming majority of people do not? After all, the superrich are just ordinary humans like everyone else. My exquisitely elegant explanation is that *they think and do things very differently as opposed to normal people*, and *they think and do those things which are fundamentally important to amassing huge fortunes extremely well.* The evidence from the world around us clearly indicates that people's financial circumstances, whether they are either fabulously well-heeled or desperately impoverished, *are a direct result of their thoughts and actions.* I want to make this crystal clear. I am saying that the superrich can attain a life of opulent luxury precisely because, and only because, of their *thoughts* and *actions.* T. Harv Eker summarizes this concept perfectly in *Secrets of the Millionaire Mind*[1] by stating that "the fruits (results) depend on the roots (thoughts and actions)."

This implies that, if you precisely copy (or "model" as it's known in neuro-linear programming) the *mind-set* (inner game) and *capabilities* (outer game) of the superrich, then you too can

---

1 Eker, T. Harv, *Secrets of the Millionaire Mind* (2005).

achieve a comparable jet-setting lifestyle. For instance, if you accurately model the mind-set and capabilities of billionaires such as Donald Trump and Warren Buffet, then you too can become a billionaire. It really is that goddamn simple!

In all likelihood, many of the superrich have learned the thought and action patterns required for amassing large amounts of money through a long and painful process of trial and error. However, I realize that you probably have neither the time, nor the inclination, to go through this long-drawn-out and time-consuming process. Therefore, I have consolidated herein a wealth of relevant knowledge as a set of easy-to-understand principles and techniques that you can apply effectively to see real results immediately.

Most people fail in life because they either don't have the correct *mind-set* (inner game) to make money and/or they lack the *capability* (outer game). In fact at least 99.9 percent of the general public are sadly lacking in both. However, if you can perfect both your inner and outer game, then anything is possible. Therefore, to help you achieve your most outlandish financial fantasies, I will show you the following:

- *Inner game: How to develop a secret agent mind-set.* Most people think that their personality is something which they are stuck with for life. They realize that they lack the mind-set required to reach the top but feel utterly powerless to change their lot, so they just accept the disposition God gave them and make the best of it.

- I will explain that, rather than being set in stone, your character is as flexible and malleable as clay. You should come to understand, on a fundamental level, that you are not your personality, and you will discover that you can utterly change your day-to-day experience of reality.

- I will explain how you can develop the optimum personality for the realization of your darkest desires. With effective application of the techniques I am about to reveal, you should experience what is known as a paradigm shift. You can begin to see and understand reality in a radically differently way. Other readers of this book have reported that this perceptual shift is so profound that they will felt like an alien encountering a new world. I call this peculiar mental state the "secret-agent psychology".

- *Outer game: How to acquire irresistible charm*. To a huge extent, winning the money race is about getting people to dance to your tune

- I will help you to get anyone, anywhere, at any time, to do absolutely anything you want. You only need to know how and to apply the techniques effectively. You could have the almost supernatural ability to totally control any human.

Does this sound like the sort of adventure you would like to embark upon? If so, then buckle up your seat belt, because this is *definitely* something I can help you with.

You might initially treat with skepticism my bold claims that I really can transform your life. However, there is already a covert network of people around the world using these techniques to rake in gargantuan stacks of cold hard cash. I will explain how you can join them in feasting at the trough.

The teachings in this book work on various different levels. Someone who only skims through the book, just picking up the main points, will gain a superficial surface-level understanding. Even this level of knowledge will deliver great benefits. However, the more astute and sophisticated reader will also uncover a *secret, esoteric message* hidden in these pages.

There are clues to this *hidden truth* in every page of the book. The reader may uncover this profound message in a sudden moment of epiphany (an "Aha!" moment) as it startlingly jumps out at them, or their unearthing of the truth may take the form of a slow journey of discovery. I am afraid I cannot tell you what this hidden meaning is; only you can discover it for yourself. The more you read and reread this book, the closer to this secret you will get, but you will not learn it until you are truly ready.

Warning: If your competitors and enemies start using this book before you do, then unfortunately you will have to watch as they get ever richer and more powerful, while you lag behind in the game of life. To avoid missing out, read this book immediately, and start acting on the advice herein straightaway.

I WILL SHOW YOU HOW TO SEE THE MATRIX

A neat analogy for the incredible journey you could experience is the outstanding movie *The Matrix*.[2] As you might be aware, *The Matrix* is an American science-fiction movie set in the near future. The hero of the story is a computer hacker called Neo. The tale begins with Neo finding peculiar and cryptic messages on his computer screen, which enigmatically refer to something known as the Matrix. He is intensely curious to discover what these mysterious communications actually signify. Despite the best efforts of the authorities to suppress his investigations, Neo eventually makes contact with a shadowy character known as

---

2 *The Matrix,* Warner Bros [1999].

Morpheus, who discloses that he can reveal the secrets of the Matrix.

Morpheus gives Neo a red pill to swallow. He explains that it can allow Neo to gain an understanding of the Matrix. Upon awakening from the slumber induced by the red pill, Neo finds himself, alongside millions of other people, in a liquid-filled container, connected to a huge and intricate electrical device.

Morpheus rescues Neo from this nightmarish scenario and brings him to a levitating spacecraft. Morpheus explains to the flabbergasted hacker that he has just caught a glimpse of the "true reality." Further Morpheus relates that the vast majority of the world's population does not experience this true reality. Instead they exist within a simulated *artificial actuality*, a form of cyberspace, where evil sentient computers were created to control and mollify the human population. This artifice, which is known as the Matrix, keeps the humans docile, while their bodies are harvested as a bioelectric energy source.

Neo is horrified to find out that he has lived in this constructed illusion since he was born. Indeed, he discovers that nearly the whole of humanity is doomed to live their lives there, unaware that they are actually living in the Matrix. Ironically they believe that this artificial reality is simply the way the world works.

Morpheus is convinced that Neo is The One, a Messiah-like figure destined to save the world. He persuades Neo to join a courageous band of rebels, known as the Free Humans. These radicals aim to unplug others from the Matrix and enlist them to fight the evil artificial intelligence which produced it. After revealing to their recruits the true nature of reality, they intensively train them to understand the fundamental essence of the Matrix and how to manipulate its physical laws. This understanding provides them with "superhuman" powers whenever they reconnect to, and reenter, the Matrix.

This film (I do recommend that you watch it, if you haven't done so already) ends with Neo making a telephone call where he vows to show the people imprisoned in the Matrix that *anything is possible*. Please keep that insightful phrase in mind when reading this book.

I fully understand that you won't accept as true anything that is fanciful or implausible. I am completely aware that you base your beliefs on cold hard facts and common sense. However, in so many ways, the Matrix is a fitting analogy for the wisdom I shall make known to you. You might already realize, like our hero Neo, that some aspects of reality don't ring true, or appear slightly fake, and that all is not what it seems. You may understand more about this later as you progress through the book.

If you successfully absorb the profound lessons which I shall reveal, your whole identity should radically change. You might lose your self-image as an ordinary person. Instead you could come to think of yourself like Neo in the Matrix, joining a select band of Free Humans. You can receive the elite combat training you need to amass real wealth.

ARE YOU READY FOR SECRET-AGENT BOOT CAMP?

I will put you through an elite program of training for success, rather like a military boot camp. In boot camp, army sergeants use various techniques to systematically deconstruct the recruit's civilian personality, which is useless in a combat environment, as a precondition for creating a warrior fit for battle.

You will undergo a comparable process. You have been intensively programmed for *financial mediocrity* through various powerful brainwashing techniques. You should soon become conscious that you have been indoctrinated. You could find this difficult to accept at first. As Mark Twain once said, "It is easier to fool people than to convince people that they have been fooled." Fortunately, effectively applying the techniques herein will systematically remove this conditioning and transform you into an elite secret agent of success. This can make you an irresistible force, unstoppable in achieving your mission to make money hand over fist.

You should recognize that you are akin to our hero Neo, destined to achieve colossal triumphs, once you are awake to the true reality and have mastered the skills needed for your mission.

- Reading Chapter One of this book is like "taking the red pill." You are likely to see the reality of wealth creation with new eyes. You may realize that all your previous beliefs about how best to bring home the bacon, like working hard, studying, and so on, are a chimera. This is a necessary precondition for what will follow.

- Reading Chapter Two (inner game) and Chapter Three (outer game), and effectively applying the techniques therein, compares to the elite combat training undertaken by the Free Humans. I will explain to you how the psychological laws of success actually work. Therefore, when you plug into the Matrix (as it were), you should wield an undefeatable advantage over the vast majority of people, who are apparently sadly deluded about how to make it in the world.

- There is nothing *actually* superhuman about this ability of course. Anybody who possesses the wisdom of these powers (and the basic level of intelligence needed to apply them properly) can brandish them to grand effect. Evidently most folks don't remotely understand the laws of success, so from *their* perspective, your ability to attract money like iron fillings to a magnet could have the weird aura of the paranormal.

- Some people will consider the techniques which I will teach you as highly controversial, but I prefer to think of them as effective, down-to-earth, gritty, and practical ideas about how to stack up the loot big time.

B DISPELLING THREE POPULAR MYTHS ABOUT SUCCESS IN SEVEN MINUTES

To achieve true success, one must first understand how it is (and how it is not) achieved. Cast your gaze over the table below, which reveals the net worth of the world's richest people:

World Position	Name	Net Worth (2012)
1	Carlos Slim Helu and family	$74 Billion
2	Bill Gates	$56 Billion
3	Warren Buffett	$50 Billion
4	Bernard Arnault	$41 Billion
5	Larry Ellison	$39.5 Billion
6	Lakshmi Mittal	$31.1 Billion
7	Amancio Ortega	$31 Billion
8	Eike Batista	$30 Billion
9	Mukesh Ambani	$27 Billion
10	Christy Walton and family	$26.5 Billion

The staggering wealth of these individuals is so astronomically huge that it's almost impossible to relate to ordinary people's lives. This simple illustration might help.[3] The richest gentleman in the world is worth $74 billion (see table above). The average US college-graduate head of household, on the other hand, is worth $226,000. This implies that you would need to add up the wealth of around 330,000 college graduates just to match the financial means of this one fellow. This number of graduates equates to a city population the size of New Orleans.

Or, looking at things from a slightly different angle, the run-of-the-mill graduate would need to live their life 330,000 times over to accumulate the same fortune as the world's most affluent person. Therefore, it is somewhat tricky for a "normal" person to even comprehend the gargantuan wealth that the superrich possess.

So how does one grab such a gigantic slice of the money cake? Most people think that making the *Forbes* Billionaires List is about getting a good quality education, working hard, and saving up. They mistakenly believe that, if they dutifully do these things, then they too can join the hallowed ranks of the superrich. This is

---

3 Domhoff, G. William, "Wealth, Income, and Power," UC-Santa Barbara Sociology Department (found at http://www2.ucsc.edu/whorulesamerica/power/wealth.html).

the famous American Dream and is also held as a matter of faith in many other societies. Unfortunately the facts of the matter suggest that it's also complete and utter bullshit!

These misconceptions in the collective mind have infiltrated the general public, even from our parents and grandparents who went through the Great Depression or the Industrial Age where people did stay with one job their whole life. However, things have changed.

Regrettably you will never become wealthy enough to buy your own private island in the Caribbean just through putting your nose to the grindstone or working your fingers to the bone or even lucking out. Don't get me wrong. I am not saying that doing these things won't help you in certain situations, but they definitely won't cut the mustard on their own.

Elements within the business and political elites in charge of large corporations may find it advantageous for you to fall for this pack of lies—hook, line, and sinker. It keeps you perpetually slaving away on their behalf, swelling their already bulging bank accounts, while they are sitting comfortably on their lazy backsides.

For that reason they use every sneaky mechanism at their disposal, including the media (especially television), institutions (such as schools and universities), and other systems (such as the police, big business, and even your parents), to implant these false beliefs in your unsuspecting psyche. Let's shine a glaring spotlight on these devious illusions one by one:

ILLUSION 1: HARD WORK WILL MAKE YOU RICH

A commonly held view is that rich people are wealthy because they've worked hard. Absolute bullshit!

Leaders of the corporate oligarchy desperately want the masses to trust that hard work is some sort of magic bullet. Once the gullible general public is hoodwinked into accepting this as true, then living a life of luxury off their backs is like taking candy from a baby. Therefore, these greedy people systematically use channels of influence, such as the media, to effectively brainwash the plebs into "thinking correctly."

The tragic misconception that hard graft plays even the smallest part in getting stinking rich is simply a product of devious social conditioning. As John Lennon once said, "If you want to get on the trail of the truth in history, follow the money."

Just considering some basic facts will help undermine this damaging indoctrination. Clearly the notion that hard work pays off is an absolute crock of lies. Indeed, you might be surprised to know that the relationship between grueling toil and success often works the other way around. Hardworking people tend to actually earn *less* than their lazier brethren. The evidence for this is staring us in our faces, but most people are blind to it:

- Although the majority of the world's population works damn hard, nearly all of them are stone broke.

- People generally work the hardest in developing countries, like Africa and Asia. In these societies, workers often toil away at backbreaking labor in the fields and in factories for more than twelve hours a day, just to put food on the table. However, individuals in the richest countries in the world per capita, such as the Western European countries (which include Luxembourg, Switzerland, and so on), often enjoy very short workweeks—around thirty-seven hours on average.[4]

- One percent of the earth's population holds 40 percent of its wealth.[5] This implies that the top one percent is forty times more affluent than the average person. But

_____

4 Source: http://stats.oecd.org/index.aspx?DataSetCode=ANHRS#.

5 Source: http://www.vanityfair.com/news/2011/05/top-one-percent-201105.

do they work forty times harder? Well, say the average person works around 50 hours per week, and there are only 168 hours in a week (around 3.5 times the average workweek). Logic obviously indicates that no one can work 40 of those fifty-hour workweeks in one seven-day period. Therefore, working longer hours clearly isn't what separates the wheat from the chaff.

- In fact, economic theory states that there is a law of diminishing returns. As effort increases, productivity and profit will inevitably fall as tiredness sets in and mistakes proliferate.

- Individuals who slog away at the hardest, most physically demanding and mentally stressful jobs, such as farmhands, cleaners, production-line operatives, and hotel and restaurant workers, take home the most meager paychecks.

- The other side of the coin is that the lucky few in very highly paid jobs, such as football players and pop stars, live the high life for minimal effort. For instance, multimillionaire footballers only train for a few hours a day. Top music artists can earn a fortune from an album which takes a matter of weeks to produce.

Therefore, if you think that you will find wealth by sweating blood through greater and greater physical and mental exertion, then you are betting on the wrong horse.

ILLUSION 2: EDUCATION WILL MAKE YOU RICH

This brings us to the second major illusion regarding wealth creation. Another widely believed fallacy is that achieving prosperity is primarily a matter of obtaining a fine education.

It is admittedly true that well-educated individuals do earn more, on average, than those who enter the work force earlier. However, this is largely because, for cultural reasons, the naturally intelligent tend to spend longer times in school than less gifted people from deprived backgrounds.

Clever people would probably earn more than their economically deprived counterparts due to their innate ability, *irrespective* of how long they stayed in school. Therefore, just because more education is *associated* with greater achievement, it doesn't mean that it is *causing* it. Therefore, we cannot reliably claim that organized systems of learning are a significant factor behind major wealth generation.

Moreover, just consider for a moment the net worth of some of the most megafamous superrich individuals in the United States. They are all university dropouts, so they are not "highly educated" in the conventional sense.[6]. But has this held them back? Not one iota.

University Dropouts	Net Wealth
Bill Gates	$59,000,000,000
Mark Zuckerberg	$17,500,000,000
Steve Jobs	$8,100,000,000

What's more, with the exception of certain specialized fields, such as law and medicine, many academically accomplished people actually earn peanuts, relatively speaking. For example, 80 percent of postdoctoral degree holders earn a net wage of less than $39,000 per year—which is around the average salary of a humble construction worker.[7]

Therefore, even if you do accept the exceedingly dubious claim that education leads to success *on average*, it is clear that many very highfliers are not well educated. Likewise, a large proportion of well-educated people don't have two pennies to rub together.

---

6 Source: http://www.forbes.com/forbes-400/gallery.

7 Doctoral degrees: The disposable academic". *The Economist*. 2010-12-18.

Therefore, the link between formal education and success is as weak as a sheet of wet paper.

ILLUSION 3: BEING LUCKY WILL MAKE YOU RICH

The final illusion about making money that I want to dispel is that amassing untold riches is all down to Lady Luck. Providence undeniably plays a part in a limited number of cases. For instance, scooping a major lottery win isn't going to do your bank balance any harm. So if you enjoy a flutter, then please indulge in the occasional lottery ticket. However, remember that the odds of winning the lottery are similar to that of lightning striking you twice—around ten million to one. Therefore, this sort of luck is too rare for a rational person to depend upon as a meaningful success strategy.

But what about the everyday kind of serendipity? For example, making a "lucky" investment decision or landing a "lucky" job? Well, in many cases, what appears to be luck, on the surface, actually isn't. Some apparently get all the breaks, but that's only because they carefully crafted those breaks for themselves.

For example, a property developer whose investment decisions have the Midas touch (i.e. everything he puts his hands on turns to gold) might appear, to the casual observer, as being the beneficiary of an extraordinary streak of good fortune. In reality his shrewd and insightful understanding of the market has allowed him to prosper handsomely. However, outside observers attribute this success to chance because they are blissfully ignorant of the incredible skills involved.

Also the green-eyed often bitterly attribute the victories of their rivals to luck because it provides succor to their own resentful feelings. All in all, success has a lot less to do with luck than you might think.

By now you should be starting to deeply question the propagated fairy tale that getting strong academic grades, clocking up the hours at work, or getting lucky are sufficient, on their own, to become rich.

In his magnificent book *Rich Dad Poor Dad*, Robert Kiyosaki explains that most people remain forever trapped in the rat race because they are bamboozled by this cock-and-bull story. They slave away their whole lives without realizing that they have fallen into this snare (they cannot "see the Matrix"). They work themselves into the ground, but their ambitions remain a painfully distant dream. They are like a hamster on a treadmill. Eventually a point in their life comes when they sadly realize that a middle-class existence is the best they can hope for.

Kiyosaki explains that the rich, who are not nearly so gullible, understand how the cookie really crumbles. This is how they are able to avoid the rat race and instead live their lives speeding ahead on the fast track, piling up the cash higher and higher.[8]

As a conscientious and diligent member of society, you might feel rather cheated and deflated once you realize the truth of the matter. It's not pleasant to discover that you have been completely brainwashed and deceived by an illusion. You might be furious that you have fallen for this dastardly ruse. If you are indeed hopping mad, then I am totally *delighted* about that! I *want* you to veritably boil with rage; it is an essential part of removing the conditioning.

This takes us on to the next stage of your training for your mission ahead. You will hear how the superrich understand the *real* rules of the game.

---

8 Kiyosaki, R., *Rich Dad Poor Dad* (2000).

C THE REAL SECRET OF BECOMING RICH, WEALTHY, AND FAMOUS

Truly intelligent people come to understand that the key to raking in the sort of dough that would make a Russian oligarch green with envy is to possess the three secret-agent personality characteristics. These are:

- Daring courage

- Ruthless determination

- Irresistible charm

To reach the most dizzying heights of human achievement, you must *courageously* go where most men would not dare tread, *determinedly* pursue your objectives, and have the hypnotic ability to *charm others* to follow your every whim. These iron clad laws of success apply across all times and ages.

But if you don't currently possess these incredibly rare psychological characteristics, does this mean that you are doomed to a lifetime of dull mediocrity and unrelenting disappointment? Fortunately, since you have wisely purchased this book, *the answer is no!*

I will describe how to use a systematic, scientific method which, if properly applied, should rapidly and fundamentally change your personality—your "inner" game—and to reflect the proper "outer" game. My intention is to quickly transform you from an ordinary Joe to an audacious, cold-bloodedly focused, and irresistibly persuasive secret agent of success. And this, my friend, is how you please the Money God.

So what the devil do I actually mean by "inner game" and "outer game"? Please allow me to explain further.

INNER GAME: YOUR PERSONALITY IS LIKE PUTTY IN YOUR HANDS

Your inner game takes place inside your mind. It is about how you see the world around you. It relates to your attitudes, beliefs about the world, and emotions—in short, your *mind-set*.

I want to help you radically transform your inner game- giving you the mind-set (daring courage and ruthless determination) needed to strike gold—*the secret-agent psychology*. The financial and psychological benefits associated with successfully applying the mentally transformational techniques in this book are potentially huge:

THE MIND-BOGGLING ADVANTAGES OF EFFECTIVELY DEVELOPING THE SECRET-AGENT PSYCHOLOGY

- Cultivate the unstoppable confidence of a big-league CEO or business tycoon. As you increasingly take on this persona, you will experience the exquisite pleasure of other people naturally following your lead in every situation (rather than you timidly obeying the wishes of others).

- As you become more and more unstoppable and invincible, you will delight in watching your earning power grow exponentially. Opportunities for creating and amassing wealth will mushroom at an extraordinary rate (you can avoid the tedium and inconvenience of existing on a mediocre income).

- Eliminate anxiety and become completely self-assured in any circumstance. You will be flabbergasted as any traces of worry and apprehension quickly evaporate.

- Forget wasting your valuable time making an effort to impress others. As supreme confidence begins to radiate from you, other people will be unable to resist flattering you and attempting to impress you (actually this might make you feel slightly uncomfortable initially, until you get used to it).

- Face danger with inhuman levels of bravery and valor (you will find it hilarious when others panic in dangerous or stressful situations while you remain sublimely calm and unperturbed).

- Develop the incredible ability of laser-like focus on your goals. Understand the intense enjoyment of steaming ahead of your less motivated business competitors (what a great feeling as you get further and further ahead!)

- Prevent misguided individuals from dictating your path in life. Take pleasure in the exhilarating freedom of becoming a fully sovereign human being. Develop the audacity to shape your own destiny and avoid living like a sheep, blindly following the herd, irrespective of whether or not it is the right thing to do.

- Experience the deep satisfaction of knowing that you are uncompromisingly concentrating on realizing your dreams (rather than feeling secretly guilty and angry about wasting time doing things that, in your heart, you don't really care about).

Most people make the mistake of thinking that they must accept their personality "as is." They don't realize that it is possible to profoundly alter it.

In reality your personality is not set in stone. It is not hard, rigid, and fixed. The human persona is essentially more like clay. It is malleable. You can mold it into an infinite range of forms. Your current character is just one form that the clay can potentially take. You can successfully fashion your nature into a different form, if you so desire and know how. If you don't like your current psychological makeup, and if it's not getting you the results you want, it is possible to simply gift yourself a new and enhanced one. You just need to know how. In other words, as you may realize, "you are not your personality," I will show you a suite of techniques which can assist you to cultivate the secret-agent psychology; the optimum personality for success.

OUTER GAME: GETTING ANYONE TO DO ANYTHING YOU WANT

"Outer game" is about how you influence the world around you. It primarily relates to the third of the three secret-agent characteristics—charm. In Chapter Three, I will provide a practical toolkit to assist you in developing this vital personality trait.

THE AMAZING BENEFITS OF SUCCESSFULLY CULTIVATING IRRESISTIBLE CHARM

- Make extravagant amounts of money quickly by working smarter instead of wasting your life slaving away for peanuts. Success will come so effortlessly that you will feel increasing astonishment at how most people "just don't get it."

- Enjoy a delightful sense of authority and confidence when exerting extraordinary influence on people. Awkward self-consciousness and embarrassment will become a distant memory.

- Ensure that *you* call the shots as opposed to depending on others for your financial security. The humiliation of sucking up to a hated boss will become a thing of the past—*you* will be the boss and have absolute control.

- Become the undisputed leader in any context. You will discover that being a dominant bigwig, rather than a sheep-like follower, turbo-boosts your sex appeal.

- Convince anyone to buy more of your products and services, and at much higher prices. You will realize with glee and amazement that, while others have to toil away to earn their daily bread, for you, making massive amounts of money is as easy as falling off a log.

- Persuade anyone to sell you anything (e.g. your fantasy home or vehicle) at a rock-bottom price. Imagine the warm feeling of satisfaction you will have when buying things ridiculously cheaply instead of foolishly squandering your hard-earned cash.

- Achieve complete relaxation and control in any social situation (forget about being unpleasantly anxious when meeting big cheeses). You will become a veritable social magnet, irresistibly drawing others toward you.

- Make the beautiful people practically beg to date you (you will never tire of the exhilarating thrill of being the most desirable person in the room).

CHAPTER SUMMARY

To recap, you have learned the following secrets in Chapter One:

- You don't have to settle for second best. If you effectively model the inner game and outer game of the superrich then you can achieve prosperity beyond your wildest fantasies

- Becoming extremely affluent has absolutely nothing to do with working hard, being lucky, or spending years in higher education

- Instead, making it big is all about acquiring the secret-agent personality: daring courage, ruthless determination, and irresistible charm

Next I will reveal inner and outer game techniques which can help you become richer than a member of the Saudi royal family. So first let's look at how to radically transform your inner mental landscape.

Chapter Two: Inner Game- The Secret-Agent Psychology

A rich rogue nowadays is fit company for any gentleman; and the world, my dear, hath not such a contempt for roguery as you imagine.

—John Gay

In Chapter Two I will provide radical techniques to fundamentally shift your personality or, in other words, your "inner game," towards the lucrative secret-agent psychology.

You need to have certain psychological characteristics to make the grade as a secret agent of success. Firstly you need to be the ultimate *daringly courageous* risk taker. You must demonstrate detached and unflustered composure in the face of terrible peril from evil villains. Secondly you must be *ruthlessly determined* to complete your assignment. You must remember that you are "one of the good guys" who stops at nothing to successfully complete your mission.

After successfully applying the techniques I shall explain in Chapter Two, you should turn out to be totally cold-blooded and determined to achieve your objectives. You should also come to be completely unruffled, tranquil, and serene about taking the sort of risks that would leave lesser men a shivering wreck. In fact you are likely to face the most extreme and arduous situations with laconic amusement. Developing these personality traits will give you the best possible chance to obtain all the fabulous wealth and adoring fame you surreptitiously crave.

A large proportion the world's most incredibly successful people—including CEOs, business tycoons, rock stars, and top political leaders—have this kind of unique psychological makeup[9]. When you successfully use the techniques in this chapter to accurately "model" (or, in other words, "replicate") this personality type, then nothing can stand in your way. As the great Tony Robbins says, "If you want to achieve success, all you need to do is find a way to model those who have already succeeded. That is, find out what actions they took, specifically how they used their brain and body to produce the results you desire to duplicate. If you want to be ... a richer person, ... all you need to do is find models of excellence."[10]

Each chapter section, illustrated in the table below, provides a set of real-world techniques to apply in your own life. Each represents one piece of the jigsaw puzzle which, when applied correctly, will help transform your thought processes to those of the secret-agent psychology.

As your inner game rapidly changes, you should feel pleasantly shocked and surprised as you realize how the world around you changes in response to you. For instance, when you walk into a

---

[9] O'Reilly, Charles A., Bernadette Doerr, David F. Caldwell, and Jennifer A. Chatman. "Narcissistic CEOs and executive compensation." *The Leadership Quarterly* 25, no. 2 (2014): 218-231.

10 Robbins, Tony, *Unlimited Power* (1986).

room, everyone may stop and notice you. You might find yourself becoming magnetically attractive to others. Everyone should look to you to take the lead and to make the big decisions. Don't take my word for it. Just follow the instructions, and find out for yourself.

Section	Theme	Fundamental Principle
A	Physical Fitness: Win and Shape Up, or Lose and Ship Out	*Boosting your physical fitness to strengthen your mental resilience*
B	Brainwave Entrainment: Retune Your Brain to the Success Frequency	*Changing your brainwaves and, therefore, your thought processes*
C	Cognitive Behavioral Therapy: Think, Do, and Grow Successful	*Fundamentally changing the way that you think and behave*
D	Psychonutrition Therapy: You Are What You Eat: So Eat Like a Winner to Think Like a Winner	*Systematically altering the chemicals and nutrients you feed your brain to modify the way you think*
E	The Mind-Body Connection: You Need a Winner's Physiology for a Winner's Mind	*Relaxing your muscles and breathing effectively to move to a different level of consciousness*
F	Autosuggestion: Your Brain Is a Computer, So Program It for Success	*Imagining (visualization) and repeating statements (affirmations) to create your optimum personality*

A PHYSICAL FITNESS: WIN AND SHAPE UP, OR LOSE AND SHIP OUT

As the Marquis de Sade once said, "Your body is the church where Nature asks to be reverenced."

Scientific evidence indicates that you need a high level of physical fitness to develop the icy calmness associated with the secret-agent psychology. However, if you are like the ill-disciplined majority of the population, you are probably below your optimum fitness level and therefore habitually more anxious and stressed when under pressure than necessary.

Think of your body as an expensive high-performance sports car. The more lovingly you care for it, the better it will perform, when you need to push it to the max. I will explain how to develop the fitness levels needed for the mega-money-making secret-agent psychology. First let's look at why fitness is so important to your mental state.

DANCING WITH DANGER

When your mind senses a hazardous situation, it secretes hormones, such as adrenaline, in response. These chemicals cause physiological changes in your body that help you cope with the threat. Your heartbeat speeds up, and your breathing gets faster. Your awareness of your environment increases, and your reflexes improve. Scientists call this effect the "fight-or-flight" response.[11] These physical reactions help you survive. They enhance your ability to mentally focus on a dangerous situation and provide you with a burst of energy so that you can react, either by fighting back or running away. Therefore, the fight-or-flight response plays a vital role in keeping you safe from dangers.

THE FIGHT-OR-FLIGHT RESPONSE IS A DOUBLE-EDGED SWORD

Unfortunately our wishy-washy modern society psychologically conditions you to experience the fight-or-flight response in so-called "socially dangerous" situations, as well as ones that are actually physically perilous.

A socially dangerous situation is one where you might experience embarrassment or a loss of face. For example,

---

11 Source: https://www.nottingham.ac.uk/counselling/documents/podacst-fight-or-flight-response.pdf.

imagine that you are pitching a business idea to a group of venture capitalists in a dragon's-den-style setup. This situation is not *physically dangerous* in any way, shape, or form, but it is however potentially *socially dangerous*. Weaknesses in your proposal may be discovered, causing the dragons to scornfully reject it. You would naturally want to avoid this shameful outcome at all costs. It would lead to a loss of social status (you would look like a prize idiot, and expose your friends and family to contemptuous ridicule) as well as losing the dragon's funding.

This is the interesting bit. Society's wicked brainwashing causes you to experience the same physiological changes in response to this imaginary *social* danger as if you were in bona fide *physical* danger. You are completely safe from a physical perspective, but your body behaves as if you are in mortal peril as a result of its conditioning.[12]

These side effects to the fight-or-flight response can sometimes seriously leave you at a disadvantage.[13] The automatic physical

---

12 Frankenhaeuser, Marianne. "A psychobiological framework for research on human stress and coping." In *Dynamics of stress*: 101-116. (1986)

[13] Kemeny, M., "The Psychobiology of Stress," Current Directions in Psychological Science Vol. 12, no. 4 (2003): 124–129.

response can make you blush as red as a beet or go as pale as a ghost. Many people experience this when they are stressed or embarrassed. It can also inhibit salivation, making your mouth bone dry. This is why people often take unusually frequent sips from a glass of water when speaking in public. Also, because the fight-or-flight response enhances your mental focus in death-defying circumstances, you often develop tunnel vision. This causes you to excessively focus on the task at hand, blocking out important information that might have helped you deal with the situation more effectively.

Returning to our dragon's den example, if presenting your groundbreaking business idea activates your fight-or-flight response, the worldwise dragons would notice this in your body language straightaway. They will start to wonder just what it is you are so anxious about. They would think, *If this person is an absolute shivering bag of nerves, then he probably lacks confidence in his own proposal, so why should we support it?* Your physical reaction to "social danger" would undermine the credibility of your sales pitch and make it less convincing, increasing the likelihood that the dragons give you the thumbs-down.

Therefore, the pesky fight-or-flight response can be a serious obstacle to you becoming the next Mark Zuckerberg. Making it in life requires you to frequently expose yourself to so-called social danger. For instance, you may need to negotiate big deals, fire staff, and network with peers or higher-ups in your field etc. If your body habitually reacts with panic in these make-or-break situations, then, over time, this will gradually erode your chances of success. The more sensitive your flight-or-flight response is to social danger, the less you will accomplish.

Evidence shows that the best performers in pressurized social situations are those with ice-cold emotional detachment and glacial composure—a suppressed fight-or-flight response.[14] Developing this unique mental state is a crucial part of the secret-agent psychology and should allow you to compete with the big boys in any walk of life.

STAY FIT TO STAY COOL

It's common knowledge that getting into shape makes you look like a million dollars, but you might not know that it also greatly strengthens your mental capacity to deal with life's toughest challenges.[15] This is because when you are fitter you operate

---

14 Dutton, K. *The Wisdom of Psychopaths* (2012).

15 Tsatsoulis, Agathocles, and Stelios Fountoulakis. "The protective role of exercise on stress system dysregulation and comorbidities." *Annals of the New York Academy of Sciences* 1083.1 (2006): 196-213.

less often in panic mode (fight or flight) and remain sublimely chilled out when big piles of shit are hitting the fan. Medical experts explain that there are several reasons for this:

- Exercise strengthens the heart muscle, so it doesn't need to work as fast. A fast heart rate is a *symptom* of the fight-or-flight response which, as we know, is activated in times of stress. If your mind notices that your heart is beating fast, it interprets this as if you are in danger, and this causes feelings of panic. Therefore, slowing down your heart rate will help keep you beautifully unruffled and composed.

- Exercise relaxes you by getting rid of excess adrenaline, the chemical that the body naturally produces in nerve-racking situations.

- Exercise makes you more physically attractive, which acts as a potent tonic for your self-esteem. Greater self-confidence helps you step up to the plate in demanding situations.

- Lastly exercise produces endorphins, which are chemicals with similar effects as morphine. This natural high makes you feel like you can single-handedly take on the world.

THE PATH TO PHYSICAL PERFECTION

Relentlessly following the fitness program below should develop your ability to stay as cool as a cucumber in even the most death-defying situations. There is absolutely no need whatsoever to squander your hard-earned cash on expensive gym equipment or a personal fitness trainer. In fact, if you own a standard tracksuit and a decent pair of running shoes, then you are ready to go!

All the exercises (push-ups, sit-ups, and so on) that I recommend you do are commonly known and a piece of cake to perform. Just searching online for the names of the exercises will bring up plenty of information on how to perform them properly.

While you get more acclimated with the training program and become fitter than the proverbial fiddle with each week that sails by, you might notice your mental processes shifting, as you become considerably more serene and brave.

Stage One: After energetically warming up, you must perform a series of tests to provide a baseline against which to measure your current fitness levels. Grab a notepad, pen and stopwatch to keep score. Please do these tests in this order:

- *The Sit-Up Test* - do as many sit-ups as you are able to do in two minutes.

- *The Push-Up Test* - do as many push-ups as you are able to do in two minutes.

- *The 1.5-Mile Run Test* - run for 1.5 miles (this is approximately 2.4 km) and time how long it takes you.

Scribble down the score for each of your tests in your notebook as a measure of how fit you are at the beginning of the program. Then record your test scores at four-week intervals, as described in the schedule below, to see how your fitness is improving. As you become an ever more extraordinary physical specimen over the course of the training program, you should see that you can do more push-ups and sit-ups while your run time decreases. Your initial tests also give you your "maximum scores," which indicate how many sit-ups and push-ups you should do as you boldly move on to the next stage of the program.

Stage Two: The next stage is to man up and keep with the program. This training program is based on the regimen that the

British Army[16] uses to whip its new recruits into shape. There are four stages to the program, each containing four weeks of exercises. Once you achieve Level 4, you have attained military level fitness. Once there, you should keep repeating the Level 4 exercises to maintain your capability (or if you are able to push yourself even further, then do so).

Do not progress to a higher level until you are able to do all the exercises at your current level. Likewise, if a week or a level of the program seems too easy for you, then feel free to skip it and move immediately to a higher level.

16
Source:http://www.theguardian.com/lifeandstyle/2008/jan/07/healthand wellbeing.fitness1.

FIRST LEVEL: BEGINNERS

Day	First Week	Second Week	Third Week	Fourth Week
Mon	• 20-min walk-jog (jog for 2 mins, walk for 2 mins, etc.) • 2 sets of 5 dorsal raises • 2 sets of 5 tricep dips • 1 set of push-ups (maximum score) • 1 set of sit-ups (maximum score) • Rest 30–90 secs between sets	• 20-min walk-jog (walk for 1 min, jog for 3 mins, etc.) • 2 sets of 6 dorsal raises • 2 sets of 6 tricep dips • 2 sets of push-ups (maximum score) • 2 sets of sit-ups (maximum score) • Rest 30–90 secs between sets	• 20-min jog (jog for 5 mins, rest for 1 min, etc.) • 3 sets of push-ups (1/4 of maximum score) • 3 sets of sit-ups (1/2 of maximum score) • 2 sets of 7 dorsal raises • 2 sets of 7 tricep dips • Rest 30–90 secs between sets	• 15-min jog • 3 sets of push-ups (1/3 of maximum score) • 3 sets of sit-ups (1/3 maximum score) • 2 sets of 8 dorsal raises • 2 sets of 8 tricep dips • Rest 30–90 secs between sets
Tues	Rest			
Weds	• 10-min	• 10-min	• 10-min	• 10-min

	warm-up • Fast run for 30 secs, rest for 2 mins, repeat 5 times • 10-min cooldown	warm-up • Fast run for 40 secs, rest for 2 mins, repeat 5 times • 10-min cooldown • Vigorous walk for 20–30 mins or row, cycle, or swim for 15–20 mins	warm-up • Fast run for 1 min, run slowly for 2 mins, repeat 5 times • 10-min cooldown	warm-up • Fast run for 1 min, run slowly for 1 min, repeat 5 times • 10-min cooldown
Thurs	Rest			
Friday	• 20-min walk-jog (walk for 1 min, jog for 3 mins, repeat 5 times) • 1 set of 5 dorsal raises • 1 set of 5 tricep dips • 1 set of push-ups	• 20-min walk-jog (jog for 4 mins, walk for 1 min, repeat 4 times) • 2 sets of 6 dorsal raises • 2 sets of 6 tricep dips • 2 sets of push-ups	• 15-min walk-jog • 3 sets of push-ups (maximum score) • 3 sets of sit-ups (maximum score) • 2 sets of 7 dorsal raises	• 25–35 min vigorous walk, row, cycle; or swim for 15–25 mins

	(maximum score) • 1 set of sit-ups (maximum score)	(maximum score) • 2 sets of sit-ups (maximum score)	• 2 sets of 7 tricep dips	
Sat	Rest			
Sun	• 20–30 mins of vigorous walking, rowing, or cycling; or swim for 15–20 mins	• 20–30 mins of vigorous walking, rowing, or cycling; or swim for 15–20 mins	• 25–35 mins of vigorous walking, rowing, or cycling; or swim for 15–25 mins	•Fitness examination • 1.5-mile timed run • Sit-ups for 2 mins to determine new maximum score • Push-ups for 2 mins to determine new maximum score

SECOND LEVEL: INTERMEDIATE

Day	First Week	Second Week	Third Week	Fourth Week
Mon	• Medium-paced run for 18 mins • 3 sets of 8 squats • 3 sets of sit-ups (maximum score) • 3 sets of 8 dorsal raises •3 sets of push-ups (maximum score) • Rest 30–90 secs between sets	•Medium-paced run for 20 mins • 3 sets of 8 dorsal raises • 3 sets of push-ups (maximum score) • 3 sets of sit-ups (maximum score) • 3 sets of 10 lunges • Rest 30–90 secs between sets	• Medium-paced run for 20 mins • 3 sets of sit-ups (maximum score) • 3 sets of 12 dorsal raises •3 sets of 12 squats • 3 sets of push-ups (maximum score) • Rest 30–90 secs between sets	• Medium-paced run for 25–30 mins • 3 sets of 14 dorsal raises • 3 sets of 14 lunges • 3 sets of sit-ups (maximum score) • 3 sets of push-ups (maximum score) • Rest 30–90 secs between sets
Tues	Rest			
Weds	• 10–15 min warm-up • High-paced	• 10–15 min warm-up • High-paced	• 10–15 min warm-up • High-paced	• 10–15 min warm-up • High-paced

	run for 1 min, rest for 1 min, repeat for 10 mins • 10-min cooldown	run for 1 min, rest for 1 min, resume for 10 mins • 10-min cooldown	run for 1 min, rest for 1 min, resume for 12 mins • 10-min cooldown	run for 1 min, rest for 1 min, resume for 12 mins • 10-min cooldown
Thurs	Rest			
Friday	• 10-min warm-up • Circuit work: 2 sets of 12 of each exercise • 10-min cooldown	• 10-min warm-up • Circuit work: 2 sets of 12 of each exercise • 10-min cooldown	• 10-min warm-up • Circuit work: 3 sets of 12 of each exercise • 10 min cooldown	• 10-min warm-up • Vigorous walk-run for 30–40 mins. Or row, cycle, or swim for 15–20 mins • 10-min cooldown
Sat	Rest			
Sun	• Vigorous walk for 30–40 mins. Or row, cycle, or swim for 15–20 mins	• Vigorous walk for 30–40 mins. Or row, cycle, or swim for 20–25 mins	• Vigorous walk for 30–40 mins. Or row, cycle, or swim for 20-25 mins	Fitness examination • Push-ups for 2 mins to determine new maximum score • Sit-ups for 2 mins to

				determine new maximum score • 1.5-mile timed run to determine new maximum time

THIRD LEVEL: ADVANCED

Day	First Week	Second Week	Third Week	Fourth Week
Mon	• Medium-paced run for 25–30 mins • 4 sets of push-ups (maximum score) • 4 sets of 12 squats • 4 sets of 12 dorsal raises •4 sets of sit-ups (maximum score) • Rest 30–90 secs between sets	• Medium-paced run for 25–30 mins • 4 sets of 14 lunges • 4 sets of sit-ups (maximum score) • 4 sets of 14 dorsal raises • 4 sets of push-ups (maximum score) • Rest 30–90 secs between sets	• Medium-paced run for 25–30 mins • 4 sets of 16 dorsal raises • 4 sets of 16 squats • 4 sets of sit-ups (maximum score) • Rest 30–90 secs between sets	• Medium-paced run for 25–30 mins • 4 sets of 18 lunges • 4 sets of 18 dorsal raises • 4 sets of sit-ups (maximum score) • 4 sets of push-ups (maximum score) • 4 sets of 12 triceps dips • Rest 30–90 secs between sets
Tues	Rest			
Weds	• 10–15 mins	• 10–15 mins	• 10–15 mins	• 10–15 mins

	of warm-up • High-paced run for 1 min, rest for 1 min, resume for 14 mins • 10-min cooldown	of warm-up • High-paced run for 1 min, rest for 1 min, resume for 14 mins • 10-min cooldown	of warm-up • High-paced run for 1 min, rest for 1 min, resume for 16 mins • 10-min cooldown	of warm-up • High-paced run for 1 min, rest for 1 min, resume for 16 mins • 10-min cooldown
Thurs	Rest			
Friday	• 10-min warm-up • Circuit work: 3 sets of 15 of each exercise • 10-min cooldown	• 10-min warm-up • Circuit work: 3 sets of 15 of each exercise • 10-min cooldown	• 10-min warm-up • Circuit work: 3 sets of 20 of each exercise • 10-min cooldown	• 10-min warm-up • Vigorous walk-run for 30–40 mins. Or row, cycle, or swim for 30–40 mins • 10-min cooldown
Sat	Rest			
Sun	• Vigorous walk for 30–40 mins. Or row, cycle, or swim for 20––25 mins	• Vigorous walk for 30–40 mins. Or row, cycle, or swim for 25–30 mins	• Vigorous walk for 30–40 mins. Or row, cycle, or swim for 20–25 mins	Fitness examination • Push-ups for 2 mins to determine new maximum score

				• Sit-ups for 2 mins to determine new maximum score • 1.5-mile timed run to determine new maximum time

FOURTH LEVEL: PROFESSIONAL (REPEAT THE EXERCISES ON A CONTINUOUS BASIS UPON ATTAINMENT)

Day	First Week	Second Week	Third Week	Fourth Week
Mon	• Medium-paced run for 30–40 mins • 4 sets of 15 squats • 4 sets of 15 dorsal raises • 2 sets of push-ups for 45 secs • 2 sets of sit-ups for 45 secs • Rest 30–90 secs between sets	• Medium-paced run for 30–40 mins • 4 sets of 15 lunges • 4 sets of 15 dorsal raises • 2 sets of push-ups for 45 secs • 2 sets of sit-ups for 45 secs • Rest 30–90 secs between sets	• Medium-paced run for 30–40 mins • 4 sets of 20 squats • 4 sets of 20 dorsal raises • 4 sets of 12 triceps dips • 2 sets of push-ups for 1 min • 2 sets of sit-ups for 1 min • Rest 30–90 secs between sets	• Medium-paced run for 30–40 mins • 4 sets of 20 squats • 4 sets of 20 dorsal raises • 4 sets of 12 triceps dips • 2 sets of sit-ups for 1 min • 2 sets of push-ups for 1 min • Rest 30–90 secs between sets

Tues	Rest			
Weds	• 10–15 mins of warm-up • Switch between high-paced running, then resting, for intervals of 1, 2, and 3 mins (12 mins overall) • 10-min cooldown	• 10–15 mins of warm-up • Switch between high-paced running, then resting, for intervals of 1, 2, and 3 mins • 10-min cooldown	• 10–15 mins of warm-up • Switch between high-paced running, then resting, for intervals of 1, 2, 3, 2, and 1 min (18 mins overall) • 10-min cooldown	• 10–15 mins of warm-up • Switch between high-paced running, then resting, for intervals of 1, 2, 3, 2, and 1 min • 10-min cooldown
Thurs	Rest			
Friday	• 10-min warm-up • Circuit work: 4 sets of 15–20 of each exercise • 10-min cooldown	• 10-min warm-up • Circuit work: 4 sets of 15–20 of each exercise • 10-min cooldown	• 10-min warm-up • Circuit work: 4 sets of 15–20 of each exercise • 10-min cooldown	• 10-min warm-up • Vigorous walk-run for 30–40 min. Or row, cycle, or swim for 30–40 mins • 10-min cooldown

Sat	Rest			
Sun	• Vigorous walk for 30–40 mins. Or row, cycle, or swim for 30–35 mins	• Vigorous walk for 30–40 mins. Or row, cycle, or swim for 30–35 mins	• Vigorous walk for 30–40 mins. Or row, cycle, or swim for 30–40 mins	Fitness examination • Push-ups for 2 mins to determine new maximum score • Sit-ups for 2 mins to determine new maximum score • 1.5-mile timed run to determine new maximum time

This exercise regimen separates the men from the boys. Individuals not accustomed to physical exertion will suffer horribly at first. However, you must be consistent with it to attain the physical fitness levels required for the secret-agent psychology. Whatever the weather—rain, snow, or sunshine—you must get outside and train. No pain, no gain! Once you get into the habit, it's all downhill from there.

Remember that there are tremendous additional benefits from

doing this training program (as is the case with any serious exercise regimen): reducing your probability of developing serious illnesses, such as cancer and heart disease, making you feel happier, and enhancing your physical appearance.[17]

17 Warburton, D., S. Nicol, S. Bredin, "Health Benefits of Physical Activity: The Evidence," CMAJ Vol. 174, no. 6 (March 14, 2006).

B BRAINWAVE ENTRAINMENT: RETUNE YOUR BRAIN TO THE SUCCESS FREQUENCY

Your brainwaves are the seeds from which your personality grows. However, like most of the general public, your mind is probably currently on a suboptimal wavelength for wealth and success. Fortunately, emerging scientific evidence suggests that you can use a little-known technique to powerfully (but temporarily) modify your brainwaves.

Think of your brain as being like a radio; you can take that chunky knob and tune it to any wavelength you like. It is possible to dial in your gray matter to a very unusual and unique wavelength; helping you to develop the potentially extremely profitable secret-agent psychology.

HIGH-SECURITY PRISONERS AND TUNING FORKS

Rather like fingerprints, no two people have the same brainwave patterns. Intriguingly, when medical professionals conduct brain scans, they find that—among villainous high-security prisoners, who are naturally determined and daring risk takers—they all usually display similar distinctive brainwaves.[18] I will share the secret of how you can use brainwave entrainment to radically modify your brainwaves and, thereby, hopefully develop this strange type of personality (not necessarily with the criminality involved of course!). Please be mindful that, like with Frankenstein, you might create a monster!

Essentially brainwave entrainment is a scientifically proven neurological method[19] which synchronizes your brainwaves to a repetitive stimulus, so that you can change them to a desired state. When applied effectively, this technique allows humans to "select their own brainwaves," in the same way that they can change their wardrobes or their hairdo to suit the latest fashions.

A simple analogy can help you understand how it works. If you strike a tuning fork, it will vibrate. If you then place it next to a similarly tuned fork, then that second fork will also start vibrating; to the same frequency of the first fork. Evidently the first tuning

---

18 Schirmann, F., "The Wondrous Eyes of a New Technology: A History of the Early Electroencephalography (EEG) of Psychopathy, Delinquency, and Immorality," *Front Hum Neurosci.* 8 (2014 Apr 17): 232.

19 Huang, T., C.Charyton, "A Comprehensive Review of the Psychological Effects of Brainwave Entrainment," *Alternative Therapeutic Health Medicine* (2008).

fork *entrained* the second one to vibrate to that identical frequency.

We can apply this tuning fork analogy to the human brain. Whenever you think, your brain produces a great deal of electrical activity in the form of neurons firing. Scientists use a machine called an electroencephalogram (EEG) to measure the frequency of the electrical current produced by these firing neurons. The EEG is used extensively in the medical profession to diagnose conditions like epilepsy, brain tumors, and strokes.

Basically the EEG measures the frequency of electrical activity in the brain in Hertz (Hz) units. The higher the frequency, the faster the brainwaves are. There is a strong relationship between the frequency of your brainwaves and your mood. For example, if you are feeling ecstatically happy, then your brainwaves will reflect this. If your mood then changed to feeling unbearably anxious, your brainwaves would also change in response. Every time your mood fluctuates, your brainwaves change accordingly. Therefore, you can think of your brainwave activity as a "window," through which scientists can look to observe your psychological state.

Egg-headed scientists categorize brainwaves into frequency

ranges.[20] The table below explains the major categories and their associated psychological effects.

Brainwave	Description
>40-Hz gamma waves	Higher mental activity, which includes perception, problem solving and fear
13–40 Hz beta waves	Normal consciousness. Associated with active concentration and focus, cognition, arousal, and feeling busy or anxious. Too much experience at this state can result in tension and worry.
7–13 Hz alpha waves	Light meditation, relaxation (while awake), daydreaming, and the feeling you get when you are waking up or drifting off to sleep. This state is the gateway between consciousness and unconsciousness.
4–7 Hz theta waves	Associated with dreams, deep meditation, and REM sleep.
<4 Hz delta waves	Loss of awareness of the body, unconsciousness, deep sleep, and very deep meditation.

---

20 Source: http://www.positivehealth.com/article/energy-medicine/brain-waves-and-altered-states-of-consciousness.

TUNE IN YOUR BRAIN TO SECRET-AGENT FM

Altering your brainwave state can generate Jekyll and Hyde style transformations in your personality. Since your brainwaves determine the way you *feel and think*, tuning your brainwaves to the correct pattern should allow you to actually *feel and think* like a suave secret agent.

Based on a similar principle to the tuning fork analogy, you can use an audio stimulus to entrain the brain to a particular frequency and so generate your desired psychological state. The free audio program which comes with this book aims to do this by using fiendishly clever audio stimuli, known as isochronic tones.[21] These are rapid pulses of sound, which are turned on and off at frequent intervals, to systematically entrain your brain. After listening to these tones for a while, the brain is entrained to the same frequency as the tone. In other words, you can use repetitive sounds to readjust your brain to the wavelength of your choice.

So how does purposefully fiddling with your brainwaves allow you to develop the secret-agent psychology? Interestingly

---

21 Doherty, C. *"A Comparison of Alpha Brainwave Entrainment, With and Without Musical Accompaniment,"* (2014).

enough, institutional studies find that those roguish felons who naturally possess this unique type of personality have a peculiarly rare and characteristic pattern of brainwaves. They usually display higher-than-average levels of theta waves. Studies show[22] that up to 58 percent of people with this personality type have increased levels of theta waves relative to the normal population. These brainwave frequencies are associated with a state of supreme extraversion and a remarkable absence of anxiety.

The science of brainwave entrainment explains that, if you alter your brainwaves to an identical range, you can then develop the exact same personality traits. This implies that developing the thought processes of a dashing secret agent is a simple matter of correctly tuning your brainwaves.

---

22 Calzada-Reyes, A., et al., "Electroencephalographic Abnormalities in Antisocial Personality Disorder," *Journal of Forensic and Legal Medicine* Vol. 19, issue 1 (January 2012): 29–34.

GET IN THE ZONE WITH ISOCHRONIC TONES

Your free audio file (which I will explain how to access at the end of the book) methodically exposes you to successively increasing levels of theta waves as the weeks of the programming progresses. As you follow the carefully calibrated schedule, like the tuning fork, your brain should increasingly exhibit brainwaves of this frequency. You should think and feel more like a cold-blooded secret agent, as you literally "tune in to the same wavelength."

Toward the end of the program, the audio file combines the brainwave stimuli with recorded autosuggestive messages. Autosuggestion packs a doubly powerful punch when the brain is operating in the theta state.[23]

To see why autosuggestion works like magic when the brain is on the theta wavelength, you need to first understand how the mind operates in its normal or everyday state (characterized by beta waves). Under normal circumstances, the conscious brain diligently filters out those autosuggestions which are not consistent with previous programming.

---

23 Jha, C., *Achieve Your Highest Potential: Be the Best You Can Be* (2012).

For example, imagine that a painfully shy person is using autosuggestion to make himself more assertive. To do this, he faithfully repeats affirmations, such as "Every day and in every way, I become more and more confident." If this person's previous programming contradicts this suggestion (i.e., he fundamentally believes that he is actually cripplingly self-conscious), then the autosuggestions are likely to fail. This is because the skeptical gatekeeper of the conscious mind suspects self-deception and refuses the autosuggestion's entry to the subconscious. Therefore, when the brain is in its normal or everyday state, gaining entry into the subliminal mind is like breaking into Fort Knox.

However, in the theta state, ideas are formed without the conscious mind censoring them whenever they do not agree with existing programming. This is because theta waves are associated with daydreaming and free-flowing thought as opposed to analytical and critical thinking. Consequently you are much more likely to accept suggestions while in the theta state. For this reason, theta is known as the "medium state of hypnosis."

Therefore, not only can you use entrainment techniques to realign your brainwaves but it also provides a free bonus prize of making autosuggestion more effective.

TURN ON, TUNE IN, AND CHILL OUT

Next I will show you how to actually go about this diabolically clever brainwave entrainment business:

- First of all, create a suitable environment for your entrainment session. Ideally you should designate a specific area in your home for this purpose. It doesn't matter whether you recline in a comfortable armchair or lie down on a bed, as long as you are physically at ease.

- You must insulate yourself from annoying distractions. Ask your dear family, on the pain of death, not to disturb you for the duration of your session. Shut the door and all the windows. Make sure your environment is clean and don't leave anything in the room that might divert you, such as a TV, computer, or radio. You might prefer a completely dark environment.

- The next step is to prepare physically for the session. Eat a little something. Otherwise, hunger pangs will provide an unwelcome distraction. Gulp down at least half a liter of water to ensure that you are reasonably hydrated.

- Allow your mind to empty itself of intrusive thoughts. A neat way to do this is to carry out a simple household task before your session, such as washing the dishes, cleaning the floor, or tidying up (your spouse will be delighted). Anything which doesn't require mental concentration or focus will work like a charm.

- You are now ready to begin the session. Listen to the appropriate audio file for your particular week of the program. These are set out in the table below. Most people prefer to use headphones to block out any background noises. Set an alarm clock so that you know when to finish.

Before you know it, the alarm clock will ring to signify the end of the session. You might feel slightly disoriented at this point. Relax for a few minutes before returning to your daily routine.

THE ROAD MAP TO AN ALTERNATE REALITY

Your entrainment program is structured so that your brainwaves should progressively change from their rather boring normal state toward the secret-agent wavelength. You might not notice the results immediately, but, over time, you should notice profound changes in your mental state. The principle here is that 'you reap what you sow'. The more sessions you do, the bigger the potential benefit.

Once you reach Week Twenty, you should have fully reset your brain. To maintain this psychological state, you need to repeat, on a daily basis, the "steady state" audio file referred to in the last row of the table below.[24]

_____

24 A couple points about the table: First of all, I make reference to the Shuman Resonance. This is the frequency of the magnetic field that surrounds the Earth. Evidence suggests that training your brain to that particular frequency has especially relaxing and refreshing properties. The table also refers to "affirmation sets." These are just groups of affirmations that we use for autosuggestion.

Week	Audio File	Frequency
1	Audio file A	12 Hz
2	Audio file A	12 Hz
3	Audio file B	10 Hz
4	Audio file B	10 Hz
5	Audio file C	7.48 Hz (Shuman Resonance)
6	Audio file C	7.48 Hz (Shuman Resonance)
7	Audio file D	7 Hz
8	Audio file D	7 Hz
9	Audio file E	frontal-midline theta from 6.2–6.7 Hz
10	Audio file E	frontal-midline theta from 6.2–6.7 Hz
11	Audio file E(R1)	frontal-midline theta from 6.2–6.7 Hz plus daring courage affirmations
12	Audio file E(R2)	frontal-midline theta from 6.2–6.7 Hz plus ruthless determination affirmations
13	Audio file E(R3)	frontal-midline theta from 6.2–6.7 Hz plus irresistible charm affirmations

14	Audio file E(R1)	frontal-midline theta from 6.2–6.7 Hz plus daring courage affirmations
15	Audio file E(R2)	frontal-midline theta from 6.2–6.7 Hz plus ruthless determination affirmations
16	Audio file E(R3)	frontal-midline theta from 6.2–6.7 Hz plus irresistible charm affirmations
17	Audio file E(R1)	frontal-midline theta from 6.2–6.7 Hz plus daring courage affirmations
18	Audio file E(R2)	frontal-midline theta from 6.2–6.7 Hz plus ruthless determination affirmations
19	Audio file E(R3)	frontal-midline theta from 6.2–6.7 Hz plus irresistible charm affirmations
20	Audio file F	frontal-midline theta from 6.2–6.7 Hz plus mixed Secret-Agent Method affirmations
Steady state	Audio file F	frontal-midline theta from 6.2–6.7 Hz plus mixed Secret-Agent Method affirmations

C COGNITIVE BEHAVIORAL THERAPY: THINK, DO, AND GROW SUCCESSFUL

A famous countercultural philosopher Robert Anton Wilson once wisely claimed that "Reality is whatever you can get away with."[25] In other words, if you believe something is true, and you act as if it's true, then it generally becomes so in reality.

To develop the potentially highly lucrative secret-agent psychology, you need to *think* and *behave* in a very particular and specific way. However, it is likely that you, as most people, will make systematic errors in your patterns of thought and behavior.

I will explain how you can use cognitive behavioral therapy (CBT) to address this problem. CBT is a well-known psychological approach[26] which corrects unhelpful emotions, thoughts, and behaviors. Mastering this powerful technique will assist you in developing the unstoppable mind-set required to make serious money.

———————————————————

25 Wilson, R. A., *Reality Is Whatever You Can Get Away With* (1996).

26 Beck. S. *Cognitive Behavior Therapy: Basics and Beyond* (2011).

101

You can use CBT to smash the repetitive cycle of everyday thinking and mentally shift into secret-agent mode. You can revolutionize your thought patterns to create an infinitely more successful and exciting way of understanding the world around you. Most people act in an unnecessarily risk-averse, fainthearted, and softheaded way. This is because they constantly make certain wealth-repelling mistakes in the way they think.

I will reveal to you three *false truths* to help you to recalibrate your thought processes for unimaginable levels of financial gain. These rules are essentially guidelines on how to think more intelligently about the world and how it works. I call them "false truths" because, although I want you to accept them as gospel for your own benefit and profit, nothing is *really* true, as I will explain. Calling them this is just my quirky little way of emphasizing this fundamental point.

To understand how the false truths work, you first need to appreciate the true nature of "reality." The peculiar fact you must grasp completely is that "reality is not real."

This may sound rather strange, so let me explain further. The common misperception is that you can use your five senses (sight, hearing, touch, taste, and smell) to comprehend "true reality." People think that they sense the world in terms of *how it really is*. For example, imagine walking through a city (say, New York or London) on a bright winter's day. While happily strolling along, you would see, hear, smell, and feel certain things. It would be easy for you to believe that the way you sense that city, what you see, what you hear, what you smell, and what you feel, is *the way the city really is*. You strongly believe that you are experiencing the "real reality."

However, the fact of the matter is that everybody experiences a *different* reality because we all perceive things in a completely unique and individual manner. I know that this sounds a bit abstract, so consider the following picture as an example. Some observers see a vase. Others see two opposing human faces.

Here is another example. In this picture, some see a young girl with her head turned to the side. Others see an old woman with a hooked nose

Whichever way you see the images, concentrate hard; you will suddenly realize that there is another way to perceive them. So which one of these perceptions is the *true* reality? The answer is *neither*, these are actually different versions of reality, and each is perfectly valid to the individual perceiving it. These cute examples illustrate a much more philosophical and profound point—that there is not one single "real reality." In other words, "truth is in the eye of the beholder."

So why does everyone perceive the world from a different vantage point? Robert Anton Wilson explains[27] that everyone lives their lives in separate "reality tunnels." Each individual's subjective experience of life is entirely dissimilar. Wilson argues that this is because people possess different mental filters.

You are constantly bombarded with a mass of information from the world around you. Since you only have a finite amount of mental "bandwidth," it is not possible to make use of all this information; so your mind subconsciously filters out much of it. This mental sifting allows you to focus on what is important and to discard the rest. What you keep and what you filter out determines your perception of reality—your "reality tunnel."

No two individuals possess identical mental filters. The type of filters that we have depends on our "imprinting"—the impact of our life experiences on conditioning our mental processes. Since our personal histories are very diverse, we all perceive a unique version of "real life." In other words, we "live in separate reality tunnels."

Let's return to our example of walking through a metropolis. First, imagine that an accomplished architect is taking the same route. His professional experiences, and how his occupation conditions him to see the world, will shape his imprinting. Therefore, his

---

[27] Wilson, R. A., *Prometheus Rising* (1983).

mental filters will predominantly focus on information relating to architecture: the style, composition, and design of the individual buildings, as well as the overall aesthetic effect of the environment. This person will filter out most of the information that doesn't relate to his beloved architecture. He is primarily in an "architectural reality tunnel."

But someone with an alternative occupational background would experience the same saunter through the city in a completely unalike way. Imagine that an eagle-eyed policeman is making this trip instead. His professional experience and training in fighting nefarious lawbreakers will fundamentally shape his imprinting. Therefore, his mental filters would focus on potential felonious activity, the security of buildings and shops, the body language of suspicious characters, vulnerable people who may become victims of criminality, and so on. The intrepid cop would mentally sift out any non-crime-related information, which he regards as being of a lower order of importance, thereby creating a "policing reality tunnel." Therefore, individuals from dissimilar professions will inhabit reality tunnels which are poles apart in terms of their subjective experience.

But of course occupation is only one piece of the jigsaw puzzle in constructing someone's reality tunnel. Religious, political, and philosophical beliefs are all highly influential. A Christian's religious beliefs will create one kind of reality tunnel. An anarchist's political beliefs will produce a totally different kind.

Essentially anything that plays a fundamental role in shaping someone's character will affect their reality tunnel.

Reality tunnels are self-reinforcing; the more an individual's mental filters home in on a particular type of input data, the more important it will seem. This will cause a greater focus on that type of info, which in turn makes it appear more significant. For example, a dogged policeman who singularly concentrates on issues relating to legal wrongdoing will see criminality everywhere he goes. This will make him believe that crime is more important than any other concern, which will cause an even greater focus on offenders and so on. Therefore, reality tunnels generate a sort of psychological self-fulfilling prophecy.

For this reason, reality tunnels are generally transparent to their inhabitants; individuals don't realize that they are living inside their own self-constructed model of the truth. The upshot of this is that they generally assume that their beliefs reflect the "one true version" of reality. It's like the Chinese story of the toads living at the bottom of the well who consider that the small patch of sky they can see is the whole world.

It is somewhat amusing to observe two people with radically different viewpoints—for example, a hard left-wing person and a hard right-wing person— debating politics. They both get quite frustrated that their debate partner doesn't share their "commonsense" view of the world. Because left-wingers and right-wingers do not have the same imprinting (experiences and conditioning), they perceive the same society from a completely different standpoint. The reason that they can't agree on the most trivial point is that they each base their arguments on profoundly dissimilar fundamental assumptions "about how things work."

Interestingly it is perfectly possible to quickly switch from one understanding of reality to another. The delightfully insightful Robert Anton Wilson argues[28] that you can ditch your old mental filters and replace them with brand-spanking-new ones. Like switching to a different TV channel, this allows you to step outside your existing tunnel and see life through an astonishing new lens. You can swap your mind-numbing current reality for whatever tickles your fancy.

My humble suggestion is that the secret of becoming richer than the Sultan of Brunei is to experience life through the reality tunnel of a debonair and ruthless secret agent. I propose that you can achieve this by internalizing the three false truths I told you about earlier and which I will list soon.

The false truths which I am about to divulge are self-fulfilling prophecies. The more strongly you believe in them, the more the universe should shift and bend to make them true in your life. Therefore, it is in your interest to accept them with the certainty.

---

[28] Ibid.

FALSE TRUTH NUMBER ONE: I ALWAYS COME UP TRUMPS

If you have an unshakable conviction that you are luckier than a field full of four-leaf clovers, then this belief should change your behavior in such a way that you will magnetically attract wealth and success. This is because:

- If you are absolutely confident that you are lucky, you will keep your eyes peeled for auspicious opportunities. The fact that you are making a more focused effort to identify these propitious offerings means you are more likely to actually stumble across them.[29]

- Robert Anton Wilson gives the example of self-fulfilling expectations of "fortunately" finding money which has been dropped on the floor. He raises the question of why some people always find money lying around on the ground and others never do. He reasons that it's all about how lucky you feel.

- If you consider yourself a charmed individual who is expected to happily chance upon some discarded cash,

---

[29] Wiseman, R., *The Luck Factor* (2004).

then you will constantly scan the ground as you stroll down the road. This makes it more likely that you will actually find some valuable coinage. But if you believe that you are the sort of ill-fated person who never finds so much as a penny, then you won't even bother glancing at the floor or ground as you walk along. This makes it very improbable that you will actually discover anything of worth. As a rule, considering yourself fortunate will open up new and lucrative doors of opportunity, which would otherwise be closed to you.

- If you regard yourself as inordinately blessed, you will adopt a chilled-out approach to life, which includes not excessively concerning yourself with what other people think of you and how to please them.[30] Since the mind and body are intimately connected, calming your mind will also act as a soothing tonic for your body. As I explain elsewhere in this book, people are irresistibly drawn, like moths to a flame, to those with relaxed body language. This is because these nonverbal signals make them feel marvelously at ease and comfortable. Therefore, seeing yourself as fortunate will make you

---

30 Ibid.

universally loved and adored, plugging you into the money-spinning social networks that really matter.

- If you see yourself as lucky, then whenever life gives you lemons, you will make lemonade.[31] You will react to disappointing situations by identifying opportunities to turn failure into success.

The law of averages dictates that everyone is likely to experience the dark shadow of misfortune at some point in their lives. If you view yourself as blessed by the gods, you will cheerfully reframe these setbacks to your own advantage and learn valuable lessons from them. A case in point is the following person who:

- Started a business which went bust

- Started another business which also went bust

- Experienced a period of depression in his late forties

- Was defeated in the US congressional and senatorial elections

---

31 Makri, S., Ann Blandford, "Coming Across Information Serendipitously – Part 1: A Process Model," *Journal of Documentation* Vol. 68, issue 5 (2012): 684–705.

This individual was no other than Abraham Lincoln.[32] At fifty-one, he was elected president of the United States. When asked about his difficult life, he always maintained that he never saw his various adversities as failures, only as openings for more success. Having unbending assurance that fate is smiling down upon you will, like President Lincoln, give you the willpower to reach the highest pinnacle of success. OK, so later he got assassinated on Good Friday, but that is a different story!

Luck breeds luck. If you consider yourself fortunate, then the doors of accomplishment should swing open for you. Continual victories should reaffirm the belief that the gods are cheering you on. This should strengthen your "lucky reality tunnel" and make you demonstrate even more of the attractive behaviors described above. You ought to then accomplish even more great things, which must certainly further fortify this lucrative mental perspective. Therefore considering yourself as lucky can help you create an unstoppable, virtuous circle of attainment.

---

32 White, R. C., *A. Lincoln: A Biography* (2014)

FALSE TRUTH NUMBER TWO: EVERYONE WANTS ME TO SUCCESSFULLY COMPLETE MY ASSIGNMENT

If you are convinced that everyone in the world is on your team and rooting for you to scoop life's rollover jackpot, then this will naturally change your behavior and help to make this true in reality.[33] This will allow you to tap into valuable social networks (remember, it's not what you know; it's who you know), and, with a bit of luck, swelling your bank balance accordingly:

- If you believe that people always like you and want to help you, then you are more likely to get to the heart of the action, socially speaking, and have the nerve to pitch yourself effectively to the real movers and shakers. For example, you will be drawn toward high-profile business events, elite parties, fashionable and exclusive venues, and so on. Over time, through a process of osmosis, you

––––––––––––––––––––––––––––

34 Miller, Dale T., and William Turnbull. "Expectancies and interpersonal processes." *Annual review of psychology* 37, no. 1 (1986): 233-256.

too should gain admittance to this highly profitable inner circle.[34]

- If you have faith that other people view you positively, you will generally feel a warm glow toward them too. Since the mind and body are one, you should display relaxed and open body language as a result. As I mentioned earlier, this can attract people to you like flies around a big pile of manure.[35]

- It is a fact of life that not all your networking attempts will bear fruit. Sometimes, despite your charming overtures, you will fall flat on your face.

- A lack of confidence could lead you to take these occasions to heart and to feel hurt, insulted, and rejected. This could make you "go into your shell" and

―――――――――――――――――――

34 Anderson, C., et al., "Status-Enhancement Account of Overconfidence," *J Pers Soc Psychol*. 103(4) October issue: 718–35. Epub 2012 Jul 16.

35 Ibid.

shy away from seeking out future networking opportunities.

- However, if you firmly believe that others see you as a veritable idol of worship, then you ought to brush away these infrequent setbacks like water off a duck's back. Instead of taking the rejection personally, you can attribute it to circumstances. Instead of thinking that *This person won't help me because he doesn't like me*, you can reason *Maybe he is having a bad day—it's no big deal.* In short, you react to occasional social failures with a nonchalant shrug of the shoulders and a wry chuckle.

- The great Tom Hopkins makes an excellent point in his classic text on how to revolutionize your sales skills.[36] He claims that the most prolific sales reps "learn to love no." This is because they develop "ego resilience"—the power to handle rejection. They learn from it and turn it to their own advantage. Salesmen without ego resilience let rejection grind them down. Eventually they give up and leave money on the table in the process.

---

36 Hopkins, T. *How to Master the Art of Selling Anything* (2010).

- Therefore, maintaining a positive mind-set about the attitudes of others toward you will help your social networks to flourish magnificently.

FALSE TRUTH NUMBER THREE: I LOVE THE EXCITEMENT OF ACHIEVING MY MISSION

If you are of the mind that life is an enjoyable escapade to be savored, rather than an onerous duty or a chore to fulfill or endure, then your day-to-day is likely to mirror this. If you have an intoxicating passion for adventure pulsating in your soul, then you ought to exhibit the daring and courageous conduct required to make big money.

- If you see life as an exciting journey, you should seek out new and exhilarating experiences at every opportunity.[37] The success mechanism works along similar lines as the cases of lucky and unlucky people searching for coins on the floor. Just as a fortunate person notices new opportunities where an unfortunate person would not, an audacious person will naturally

---

37 Zuckerman, M. *Behavioral Expressions and Biosocial Bases of Sensation Seeking* (1994).

follow the signposts marked "adventure," while a more timid individual would look or walk the other way. Over time the adventurer will reap dividends, as fortune always favors the bold.

- Imagine that you lose your job. If your purpose in life is a dismal and fearful effort to avoid risk at all costs, then this situation would completely depress you, because your income is no longer certain.

- However, if you are brave enough to laugh in the face of danger and uncertainty, you will see your change in circumstances as the beginning of a wonderful new chapter in your life. For example, you might consider the thrilling possibilities associated with setting up your own business. If you face life with a buccaneering spirit, then, over time, you can propel your financial situation into a completely different orbit.

- Exhibiting a plucky and dauntless attitude toward life should inevitably bring you into contact with like-minded spirits. Birds of a feather tend to flock together. For example, dynamic entrepreneurs usually know a lot of other dynamic entrepreneurs. High-flying executives typically network with other high-flying executives. Mixing in the right circles will help you stride down the path to a celebrity lifestyle.

D PSYCHONUTRITION THERAPY: YOU ARE WHAT YOU EAT, SO EAT LIKE A WINNER TO THINK LIKE A WINNER

Have you ever heard the phrase "garbage in, garbage out"? Well, that statement is certainly true regarding what you eat and drink. It is a well-known fact that if you drink beer or coffee, those beverages will significantly change your mental state. Guzzling down a couple beers makes you pleasantly relaxed and talkative. Gulping down coffee gives you a mentally energetic and focused buzz. But did you know that practically anything you eat or drink profoundly influences how you think and feel?[38]

Like most people, you probably underconsume those substances which can turbocharge your brain for success while overconsuming other ingredients, most of which shroud your wits in a fog of lethargy. This bad diet is literally poisoning your mind and preventing you from amassing the huge wealth that you truly deserve.

---

38 Fredericks, C., *Psychonutrition* (1976).

Pharmaceutical science is increasingly sophisticated in its understanding of how the nutrients you derive from your diet affect the health and effectiveness of the brain as an organ. I will tell you about the substances which are most important in creating the wealth-attracting secret-agent psychology, ruthlessly eliminating those substances that make you nervous and stressed, and supplementing with those which make you cool, chilled out, and in command of any situation.

CAFFEINE: LIQUID STRESS

Caffeine is a regular part of most Western people's diet. It is most popularly consumed as coffee and tea. Folks like drinking these beverages because they temporarily improve mood and energy. This benefit occurs because caffeine blocks receptors for adenosine, a brain chemical which prevents the body from creating two other substances, known as dopamine and adrenaline, which both temporarily boost feelings of well-being.

But caffeine is a double-edged sword. Activating this chemical response on a daily basis can eventually make you horribly nervous and strung out. In fact the mental effect of caffeine is almost chemically indistinguishable from that of stress and anxiety. There is no such thing as a free chemical lunch- if you want to experience the upside from drinking caffeine then you have to accept the downside too.[39]

As you know, the economically advantageous secret-agent psychology requires you to react to any situation with total emotional calm and absolute mental relaxation. Since, as the explanation above implies, caffeine prevents you from achieving this mindset, you should mercilessly eliminate caffeine products from your daily diet.

SUGAR: THE SICKLY POISON

Sugar is another substance which significantly contributes to nervousness and tension. Eating comfort food, like cakes and sweets, is initially rather gratifying. This is because the body quickly absorbs the sugar that those foods contain and converts it into glucose molecules. This creates uplifting and pleasant

---

39 Sawyer, D. A., H. L. Julia, and A. C. Turin, "Caffeine and Human Behavior: Arousal, Anxiety, and Performance Effects," *Journal of Behavioral Medicine* 5(4), (1982): 415–439.

emotions. Blood sugar levels are elevated at this point but, after a short period of time, the body disposes of the sugar, which it treats as a poison, as quickly as possible. This creates a rebound effect, leading to a brutal crash in blood sugar levels.

This plunge in blood sugar often causes stress and irritability. These negative emotions create a desire for more sugar to maintain the previous "high." Eating more of it leads to another spike in blood sugar and so on. Sugar consumption creates profoundly unstable blood sugar levels. This volatility, in turn, creates excess adrenaline, triggering the fight-or-flight response and sending the brain into panic mode.[40] Therefore, if you want to think like Mr. Bond himself, you should eliminate sugar from your daily diet to conquer anxiety and worry.

---

40 Souza, C. G., et al., "Highly Palatable Diet Consumption Increases Protein Oxidation in Rat Frontal Cortex and Anxiety-Like Behavior," *Life Sciences* 81(3), (2007): 198–203.

5-HTP: THE LEGAL LOVE DRUG

The element 5-HTP[41] is derived from the amino acid tryptophan. It produces the neurotransmitter serotonin as well as contributing to the production of the thyroid hormone, which boosts energy-producing cells. The consumption of 5-HTP can deliver the following beneficial effects:

- Make you feel upbeat and positive

- Improve motivation levels

- Provide a physical boost

- Increase self-confidence and reduce anxiety

- Reduce cravings for food

- Increase sleep quality

- Reduce sensitivity to pain

---

41 Kahn, R. S., et al., "Effect of a Serotonin Precursor and Uptake Inhibitor in Anxiety Disorders: A Double-Blind Comparison of 5-Hydroxytryptophan, Clomipramine and Placebo," *International Clinical Psychopharmacology* 2(1), (1987): 33–45.

Please *do not* combine 5-HTP with antidepressive drugs, as this can cause unpleasant medical side effects.

TAURINE: IT'S NO BULL

Taurine is derived from the amino acid cystiene. It is one of the main neurotransmitters, and its role is to calm your emotions and reduce stress.[42] Many energy drinks use this ingredient to soothe and offset the jittery feeling associated with their high-caffeine content. Taurine also causes the brain to absorb other anxiolytics (relaxing nutrients), such as magnesium, more effectively. Taurine can generate the following psychological advantages:

- Increase feeling of calmness

- Improve sleep

- Reduce anxiety

---

42 Zhang, C. G., S. J. Kim, "Taurine Induces Antianxiety by Activating Strychnine-Sensitive Glycine Receptor in Vivo," *Annals of Nutrition & Metabolism* 51(4), (2006): 379–386.

GLUTAMINE: THE GABA GIVER

Taking the amino acid glutamine is like giving your brain a delicious bowl of strawberries and cream. Most important it produces the neurotransmitter GABA (which is also an amino acid). This stimulates the production of alpha waves, which should elevate you to a state of calming bliss.[43] Glutamine can also dampen cravings for alcohol and other drugs due to the increase in GABA and enkephalins. Glutamine can lift your mood in the following ways:

- Reduce tension

- Reduce anxiety and increase calm

- Increase sleep quality

- Improve self-confidence and self-security

In some countries it is possible to buy GABA in its pure form, rather than taking glutamine. It is perfectly acceptable to do this.

---

43 Lydiard, R. B., "The Role of GABA in Anxiety Disorders," *The Journal of Clinical Psychiatry* 64 (2002): 21–27.

However, *you should avoid taking more than 3000 g of pure GABA per day*, as it can cause shortness of breath and (counterintuitively) anxiety at high doses.

METHYL NUTRIENTS: YOUR BODY'S AIR TRAFFIC CONTROLLER

Whether you boast a healthy brain, and, therefore, a hearty mental attitude, often depends greatly on the effectiveness of a chemical process known as methylation. This process is very important for producing neurotransmitters and keeping them in balance. It is also vital for producing brain cell membranes. To use a metaphor, if you think of your body as an airport, then methylation is the air traffic controller, making sure everything runs smoothly. Ineffective methylation means that your brain will not properly convert amino acids into neurotransmitters (the airplanes will crash!). These are the most important methyl nutrients:

- B Vitamins, which include:

  - Vitamin B_2 (riboflavin)

  - Vitamin B_3 (niacin or niacinamide)

- Vitamin B_6 (pyridoxine, pyridoxal, pyridoxamine, or pyridoxine hydrochloride)

- Vitamin B_9 (folic acid)

- Vitamin B_{12} (various cobalamins, which are commonly known as cyanocobalamin in vitamin supplements)

- Magnesium

- Zinc

Supplementing with these nutrients will improve methylation, which ought to provide the following psychological perks:[44]

- Increase energy

- Improve mental clarity and concentration

- Raise mood and promote optimistic thinking

- Reduce colds and physical ailments

----

44 Holford, P., *Optimum Nutrition for the Mind* (2010).

- Improve sleep quality

- Ease muscle tension

- Reduce insomnia

- Diminish muscle cramps

- Reduce craving for nicotine, caffeine, and drugs

OMEGA 3: MAKES GRAY MATTER FATTER

The infamously unhealthy modern Western diet—which is high in substances such as caffeine, nicotine, and alcohol—leads to woefully inadequate levels of the essential fats (Omega 3 and Omega 6).

Aside from increasing the risk of heart disease, cancer, stroke, and diabetes, the reduced levels of these essential fats can also seriously jeopardize your mental health. There are two reasons for this. First, brain scans show that the more essential fats an individual regularly consumes, the denser the gray matter they have in the area of the brain which regulates mood levels, especially the part of the brain known as the hippocampus. Second, consuming essential fats lifts dopamine and serotonin levels. Evidence suggests that essential fats can provide the following mental benefits:[45]

- Quash anxiety

- Quell irritability

- Enhance memory function

- Heighten general mental performance

- Lift mood

VITAMIN C: THE RAT CATCHER

You need to stock up with vitamin C to keep your brain in tip-top condition. Remember those neurotransmitters I told you about, the ones that regulate mood and make us feel cheerful and relaxed? The brain will only produce enough neurotransmitters if it is protected from assault from the sinister entities known as free radicals (otherwise known as oxidants), which attack the

---

45 Kiecolt-Glaser, J. K., et al., "Omega-3 Supplementation Lowers Inflammation and Anxiety in Medical Students: A Randomized Controlled Trial," *Brain, Behavior, and Immunity* 25(8), (2011): 1725–1734.

brain's neurons. Vitamin C acts like a rat catcher, hunting down and destroying the verminous free radicals,[46] which will let the feel-good chemicals flood your brain.

THE RECIPE FOR A FREAKISHLY EFFECTIVE BRAIN

The following tables explain the substances which you should include in, or exclude from, your diet to help achieve the secret-agent psychology. You can see that taking one standard multivitamin, one standard multimineral, and a vitamin-B-complex supplement will give you sufficient levels of most of these commonly available ingredients.

---

46 Martin, A., et al., "Effects of Fruits and Vegetables on Levels of Vitamins E and C in the Brain and Their Association with Cognitive Performance," *Journal of Nutrition, Health & Aging* 6, no. 6 (2001): 392–404.

TABLE 1

Substance/Unit	Daily Dosage	Source
Vitamin A	2250 mcg	Multivitamin
Thiamin (Vitamin B_1)	10 mg	Multivitamin & Vitamin B Complex
Riboflavin (Vitamin B_2)	15 mg	Multivitamin & Vitamin B Complex
Niacin	25 mg	Multivitamin & Vitamin B Complex
Pantothenic Acid	100 mg	Multivitamin & Vitamin B Complex
Vitamin B_6	40 mg	Multivitamin & Vitamin B Complex
Vitamin B_{12}	25 ug	Multivitamin & Vitamin B Complex
Vitamin C	2000 mg	Separate supplement
Vitamin D	15 mcg	Multivitamin
Vitamin E	100 iu	Multivitamin
Biotin	50 mcg	Multivitamin
Folic Acid	500 ug	Multivitamin
Zinc	10 mg	Multimineral

Trimethylglycine TMG	1 g	Separate supplement
N-Acetyl Cysteine NAC	500 mg	Separate supplement
Calcium	200 mg	Multimineral
Magnesium	150 mg	Multimineral
Chromium	20 mcg	Multimineral
Selenium	25 mg	Multimineral
Manganese	2.5 mcg	Multimineral

TABLE 2

Substance/Unit	Daily Dosage	Source
Omega 3	2000 mg	Separate supplement
5-HTP	200 mg	Separate supplement
L-Glutamine	2000 mg	Separate supplement
Taurine	2000 mg	Separate supplement
Sugar	ABSTAIN	N/A
Caffeine	ABSTAIN	N/A

E THE MIND-BODY CONNECTION: YOU NEED A WINNER'S PHYSIOLOGY FOR A WINNER'S MIND

Everyone knows that the mind controls the body. Your mind decides to get up from your chair and walk across the room, and your body responds to its wishes, or your mind chooses to start whistling and your body follows its orders.

But most people don't realize the immense impact that the body has on the mind. The idea that the mind and the body are a single entity was first proposed by Parmenides in the fifth century BC and was later championed by the legendary seventeenth-century philosopher Baruch Spinoza. Modern-day scientists also find compelling evidence of a "mind-body connection"[47] which pervades numerous aspects of our lives.

I will explain how to enter a whole new world of physical and mental relaxation using the techniques of progressive muscle relaxation (PMR) and diaphragmatic breathing, helping you to develop the money-making secret-agent psychology.

---

47 Pally, R., "Emotional Processing: The Mind-Body Connection," *International Journal of Psychoanalysis* (1998).

THE MIND AND BODY ARE ONE

The mind-body connection works through two mechanisms.[48]
The first is that your thoughts and emotions influence your
physical state. For example, if you daydream about your favorite
food, then your mouth could start greedily watering in
anticipation of eating that tasty fare. If you feel horrendously
nervous about an upcoming important exam, you might
experience "butterflies" in your stomach. If you find yourself in an
utterly *terrifying* life-or-death situation, your hair on your arms
and neck could literally stand on end. These are all examples of
how the mind (i.e., how you think and feel) actually causes your
body to change physically.

The mind powerfully affects the body in myriad ways. In fact the
influence of the mind over the body is so strong that it can
actually profoundly affect your health. For instance the emotions
of happiness and love can actually increase t-cell production,
which boosts your immune system and prevents illness.[49]

---

48 Bunge, M., *The Mind-Body Problem: A Psychobiological Approach*
(2014).

49 Khansari, D. N., A. J. Murgo, R. E. Faith, "Effects of Stress on the
Immune System," *Immunology Today* 11 (1990): 170–175.

However, it works the other way around as well. The second mechanism (which I focus on here) is that your body is also the master of your thoughts and emotions.

A case in point, as I already explained in Section A, is how general physical exercise benefits your psychological state. Sexual intercourse (a particular type of physical activity) is associated with a whole host of desirable psychological benefits. For example, scientists found that individuals who had sex more frequently experienced less anxiety in "high-stress situations," such as public speaking. Sex is also known to improve production of the "love hormone" (oxytocin), which generates passionate feelings, trust, generosity, and emotional bonding.[50]

Your body language also greatly impacts your mental condition. Try this experiment. First copy the body language of "Mr. Painfully Anxious" for three minutes:

- Tense up your muscles

- Breath in and out rapidly—this is known as hyperventilating

---

50 Source: https://www.psychologytoday.com/blog/love-and-gratitude/201310/oxytocin-the-love-and-trust-hormone-can-be-deceptive.

- Clench your teeth hard

- Hunch up your shoulders

- Put your hands over your crotch

- Push your eyebrows together in the middle (frown)

- Fidget about

You should notice that you start feeling as nervous as a serial killer who has been pulled over for speeding. Now, for the next three minutes, mirror the body language of "Mr. Completely Chilled":

- Relax each of the muscles in your body in turn: your arms, hands, shoulders, feet, neck, and head. Feel all the tension draining out of your muscles.

- Breath slowly, steadily, and regularly

- Let your arms and hands hang loosely at your sides

- Smile

- Look around with a relaxed gaze

You might now begin to feel like the coolest cat in town. This experiment is a simple but compelling example of how your physical behavior affects your psychology.

Two specific physical behaviors are major drivers of your mental state: the way you breathe and the extent to which you habitually relax your muscles. I will show you how to do these things with optimal effectiveness, which will help you to think like a highly capable secret operative.

BREATHE LIKE BOND TO THINK LIKE BOND

There are two types of breathing. The first type is known as thoracic breathing.[51] This involves gasping shallow and rapid breaths directly from the chest. People breathe like this when they are "flapping"– reacting anxiously to a stressful situation. This is because, when the pressure is on, the flight-or-fight response pumps out adrenaline, which accelerates lung function. Therefore, thoracic breathing is "anxious breathing."

So anxiety causes breathing changes, but the relationship works the other way around as well. If you breathe from the chest, it can actually make you feel more fearful. This is because this

---

51 Source: http://www.normalbreathing.com/index-chest-breathing.php.

type of respiration destabilizes the balance between carbon dioxide and oxygen in the body. This causes your muscles to tense up and your heart to beat like a drum because your blood is insufficiently oxygenated. These physical changes trick your body into thinking that you are in a stressful situation, which in turn causes panic.[52]

If you want to remain as cold as ice, even in the face of mortal peril, then a better alternative is to use effectively diaphragmatic breathing,[53] which involves sucking in deep breaths from the abdomen. Diaphragmatic breathing is "relaxed breathing," and you should use it to help you think like an elite MI5 agent. Follow these instructions to breathe diaphragmatically:

---

52 Lum, L. C., "Hyperventilation and Anxiety State," *Journal of the Royal Society of Medicine* 74(1), (1981): 1.

53 Hazlett-Stevens, H., M. G. Craske, *Breathing Retraining and Diaphragmatic Breathing : General principles and empirically supported techniques of cognitive behavior therapy* (2009): 166.

- Breathe out

- Place one hand on your heart. Place your other hand just underneath your rib cage so that, when you start to breathe, you can feel your diaphragm move.

- Close your mouth. Breathe in slowly through your nose. If your nose is blocked for some reason (e.g., you are suffering from a virus), then breathe in through your mouth instead but with your lips pursed. The idea of using the nose, or pursed lips, to inhale is to slow down your respiration.

- While you inhale, push out your stomach. You should experience the sensation of your stomach filling up with air. You will feel your belly expand with the hand that you have placed under the rib cage. Keep the hand on your chest still. Make sure that you relax your stomach muscles while doing this.

- Even once you fill your belly, keep on breathing in. Feel the middle of your chest filling up with air. You should notice the hand on your heart moving as your rib cage and chest swell.

- Now begin to breathe out. You should do this gradually, either through your nose or through pursed lips (to slow down your breathing). As you are exhaling, allow your chest and rib cage to relax, but keep the hand on your chest motionless. When you have expelled nearly all of your breath, suck in your stomach to force out the remaining air.

Keep repeating this cycle of breathing in and breathing out. Do not leave a gap between inhaling and exhaling. Your breath should mimic a pendulum, swinging leisurely from one side to another. As soon as the pendulum reaches one side, it swings immediately back to the other side. Similarly your breath should move in and out smoothly with no pauses.

HOW TO PLAY A DEVIOUS TRICK ON YOUR BRAIN

Systematically relaxing your muscles can also prevent over-activation of the fight-or-flight response, allowing you to stand firm when the going gets tough. When the shit hits the fan, your muscles will contract in readiness for battle or retreat. If your muscles are overly tense, your body automatically puts itself on a war footing. This floods your system with anxiety-provoking adrenaline.

The progressive muscle relaxation (PMR) technique prevents this adrenaline reaction from occurring through mimicking a state of ultralow adrenaline by relaxing muscles to an exceptional degree. Used correctly, this technique cunningly "tricks" the mind into a state of complete calmness, no matter how arduous the situation, allowing you to think like a dashing secret agent.

The PMR approach is based on a fundamental characteristic of muscle physiology. If you apply tension to a muscle and afterward remove that tension, then that muscle will automatically relax. However, it actually relaxes to a greater degree than before the tension was applied, so if you tense and relax all the muscles of the body in turn, then the body will end up more relaxed than before you started.

This is how it's done: First tighten a particular muscle for about ten seconds. You should tense the muscle hard enough to feel the pressure but not hard enough to cause actual pain. Concentrate on the tension that you feel slowly building in the muscle and visualize this tension in your mind's eye. Then suddenly relax the muscle.

Enjoy, for around fifteen seconds, the beautifully peaceful feeling that this gives you. Maintain your concentration on the muscle. Notice the considerable difference in sensation between when the muscle was tightened and now, when it is relaxed. As you relax the muscle, repeat a suitably calming phrase to yourself. For example, you could say, "The tension is draining away," or "All is good," or "I am feeling more and more relaxed," or "It's all OK." Anything suitably hippie or New Age will work great.

Repeat this process for all the major muscles of the body in turn. If any particular muscle group is especially hard and knotted, then repeat the "tighten and relax" process as many times as you'd like. For example, the neck and the shoulders are often especially prone to tension, so you might want to tighten and relax them several times.

- Face
- Right hand
- Right arm
- Left hand
- Left arm
- Right foot
- Right leg
- Left foot
- Left leg
- Buttocks
- Chest
- Abdomen
- Lower back
- Shoulders
- Neck

F AUTOSUGGESTION: YOUR BRAIN IS A COMPUTER, SO PROGRAM IT FOR SUCCESS

The last part of your inner game training is discovering the strange psychological technology of autosuggestion. The brain is easily the most powerful computer ever invented, and the more intelligently you code its operating software, the more magnificently effective it becomes. I will reveal how you can place yourself on the path to tremendous wealth through systematically programming your subconscious brain with the secret-agent psychology.

We all *unintentionally* program our minds every day without even realizing it. But just like no two people have the same fingerprints, everybody programs themselves in a slightly different fashion.

Like the rest of the masses, you have probably fallen into the deadly trap of inadvertently programming yourself with bad coding. For instance, you might think or imagine things like *I don't possess the ability to get really rich* or *I am only capable of achieving middle-class respectability.*

Over time, these toxic beliefs often morph into self-fulfilling prophecies. They constrain your behavior, which in turn confirms and strengthens your original self-limiting encoding. Bad programming is pure poison for the aspiring billionaire.

Another way to think of your mind is like a garden. You must plant and carefully nurture the beautiful plants you wish to grow (positive thoughts). Otherwise, horrible weeds (negative thoughts) will thrive instead. Autosuggestion is all about sowing the right seeds in your mental garden. As Napoleon Hill states in *Think and Grow Rich*: "Every man is what he is because of the *dominating thoughts* which he permits to occupy his mind."

I will explain how to code yourself with the cyborglike thought processes of a remorseless, wealth-seeking secret agent.

ANY IDEA EXCLUSIVELY OCCUPYING THE MIND TURNS INTO REALITY

Autosuggestion is the subject of many bestsellers, including Napoleon Hill's groundbreaking *Think and Grow Rich*, which has sold millions of copies and which many high-net-worth individuals have hailed as the holy grail of self-development.

The genius French apothecary Émile Coué invented the principle of autosuggestion at the turn of the twentieth century. Dr Coué's crafty habit was to occasionally praise the effectiveness of the medicine he prescribed to his patients. He would hand out small written notes for particular remedies, lauding their miraculously restorative properties.

He noticed that when he praised a particular treatment, it was considerably more successful at curing patients than when he just gave it to them without further comment. This phenomenon was later termed the "placebo effect." Coué's findings prompted him to develop the principle of autosuggestion. He later released a seminal work called *Self-Mastery through Conscious Autosuggestion* in 1922 in the States. Coué succinctly described his method as follows:

"An instrument that we possess at birth, and with which we play unconsciously all our life, as a baby plays with its rattle. It is, however, a dangerous instrument; it can wound, or even kill you, if you handle it imprudently and unconsciously. It can, on the contrary, save your life when you know how to employ it consciously".

He made the startling discovery that using autosuggestion to manipulate the subconscious mind could treat the most gruesome and intractable diseases. Therefore, he persuaded his patients to constantly repeat the phrase, "Every day, in every way, I'm getting better and better," to cure their ailments.

His theory is that if one habitually repeats particular phrases as a mantra and consistently visualizes certain images in the eye of one's mind, then eventually the spongelike subconscious will absorb them. Almost as if by magic, physical reality should then begin to mirror these thoughts.

A PLEASANT STROLL ACROSS FLAMING-HOT COALS

The ancient ritual of fire-walking illustrates the formidable power of autosuggestion beautifully. This practice involves walking barefoot over a strip of red-hot embers or coals. Fire-walking has a prehistoric history, stretching back at least as far as 1200 BC in Iron Age India. Early cultures fire-walked as a trial of a warrior's bravery, especially during major rite-of-passage ceremonies or to test religious faith.

In more prosaic modern times, corporate organizations often include fire-walking sessions in training events to cultivate a participant's self-confidence and demonstrate the incredible power of autosuggestion.

Imagine for a moment that you are standing at the edge of a fire-walk strip. Your colleagues are waiting nearby, watching you intently. Your feet are completely bare. You glance down apprehensively at the strip of scorching-hot coals in front of you. It is at least four yards long and a yard wide. The instructor informs you that he will count down from ten and then you must walk straight across the burning coals. Are you brave enough?

Actually many thousands of plucky souls brave the fire-walk every year without suffering the slightest of burns. So how do they escape unscathed? Some people mistakenly think that fire-walking involves a kind of supernatural force or the power of "mind over matter." However, practically minded scientists know that it is actually the amazing power of autosuggestion which prevents the acrid smell of burned flesh from wafting through the air. It is simply a matter of pure self-belief.

Before facing the fire-walk, participants are trained to use autosuggestion to totally persuade themselves, in the darkest depths of their subconscious, that the coals are actually not very hot. They spend several hours repeating mantras such as "The coals are as cool as moss," and visualizing themselves walking safely across and proudly reaching the other side. Therefore, when the participants actually do the fire-walk for real, they boldly walk across the coals in a state of absolute fearlessness.

This state of complete self-confidence actually makes the fire-walk quite a harmless experience. Coal is a rather poor conductor of heat, meaning that it isn't as roasting hot as you might think. Also someone who walks at a steady pace does not usually have their feet in contact long enough with the coals to cause burns. Therefore, anyone who walks calmly and resolutely across, with a positive frame of mind, isn't really in much physical danger. Their relaxed mental state makes them safe.

Those participants who get burned do so because they haven't effectively used autosuggestion to suppress their natural feelings of anxiety and fear. When someone suddenly loses their nerve while walking across the coals, they usually freeze on the spot or try to run across, rather than walk as they are supposed to. Freezing like a rabbit in the headlights causes terrible injuries, because the feet stay in contact with the hot coals for a longer period of time. Likewise, running pushes the feet down deeper into the embers, resulting in burns to the tops of the feet.

Incidentally twenty Kentucky Fried Chicken employees were treated in a hospital for serious injuries received while participating in a fire-walk. This led to the unfortunate newspaper headline of KFC Bosses Aren't Chicken, But They Sure Are Tender![54]

The practice of fire-walking speaks to the general principle that if you consistently and systematically program yourself with certain concepts, then you will eventually internalize them on a subconscious level, changing your behavior and, in turn, your reality itself.

I will reveal how to methodically use autosuggestion to program yourself with the secret-agent state of mind. The basic concept is

---

54 Source:
http://www.theage.com.au/articles/2002/02/27/1014704967158.html.

for you to systematically suggest and imagine yourself as a ruthlessly determined, irresistibly charming and daringly courageous risk taker. Over time, successfully using autosuggestion should percolate through to your subconscious to dramatically change you into such a person.

YOU ARE WHAT YOU SAY YOU ARE

Using affirmations (consistently repeating specific phrases) is an almost magically effective technique. The four affirmations you need to regularly repeat to attain the secret-agent psychology are:

- *"I am becoming a daring and remorseless secret agent of success."*

- *"More and more, I find that I can get whatever I want."*

- *"I increasingly realize that nothing can faze me."*

- *"I am becoming unstoppable in achieving my mission."*

Say each of these phrases five times at these three points in the day: before you take breakfast, shortly after lunch, and just before you tuck yourself into bed at night. Interestingly the affirmations that you utter in the morning and before bedtime should have the biggest potential benefit on your psychological

148

state. This is because of the excess amount of alpha and delta waves which characterize the transition from wakefulness to sleep and vice versa. When you are groggily waking up in the morning or are woozily nodding off to sleep, your mind is at its most susceptible, which makes the affirmations pack a more powerful punch.

You can also repeat the affirmations at other times of the day to gain an additional advantage, if you so desire. A fiendishly clever little ruse is to wait for an occasion which presents evidence that the affirmation is indeed true and then repeat it at once to reinforce the positive programming.

For instance, imagine that you wish to program yourself with the phrase "*I increasingly realize that nothing can faze me.*" To turbocharge its effectiveness, patiently wait for a situation in which you are naturally feeling like you don't have a care in the world. This could be when you are pounding away your problems in the gym, wining and dining with good friends in a fabulous restaurant, chilling out at home while listening to some excellent music, or whatever floats your boat. Take a moment and immediately and confidently declare this affirmation. This technique works like a charm, because the subconscious brain is more likely to absorb affirmations when presented with immediate evidence of their truthfulness.

You must remember that it's not just *what* you tell your subconscious mind, it's *how* you say it too. You should boldly proclaim these affirmations like a fiery fundamentalist preacher quoting scripture. You should chant them out loudly, positively, and with burning emotion and conviction.

YOU ARE AS YOU IMAGINE YOURSELF

Another heavy-hitting autosuggestion technique to help you attain the secret-agent psychology is to systematically *visualize* yourself as a smooth undercover operative. In other words, you "put yourself in the shoes" of a fictional secret agent, mentally creating an exhilarating adventure movie where you are the star of the show.

Doing this is wonderfully simple. Each week, sit down comfily, grab some tasty popcorn, and enjoy a movie about a daring secret agent. Then for the rest of that week, imagine yourself to be that character in these films in terms of:

- The way they walk and move their body

- The way they talk (e.g. the language and tone of voice they use)

- The way they understand the world (i.e. their beliefs and values)

- The way they think and act

- *Why* they think, act, walk, talk, and move the way they do

Examples of secret agents to channel include:

- Jason Bourne from *The Bourne Trilogy*

- James Bond of 007 fame

- Agent J from *Men in Black*

- Napoleon Solo from *The Man from U.N.C.L.E.*

- George Smiley or Alec Leamas from the John le Carré novels

- Ethan Hunt from *Mission Impossible*

- Jack Bauer from *24*

- Jill Munroe from *Charlie's Angels*

I know this might sound like a rather silly idea, but just swallow your pride, and do it nevertheless. It's better to be a bit daffy and filthy rich than sensible and poor. Over time you should change into a dashing undercover operative yourself.

ASSOCIATED VERSUS DISSASSOCIATED VISUALIZATION

When you are doing visualizations, you can either be "associated" or "disassociated." When imagining you are a secret agent, if you see things through your own eyes, then you are *associated*. An alternative approach is to *disassociate*. This involves imagining yourself doing one of the following things:

- Floating out of your body and looking down on yourself from above

- Watching yourself on a TV or cinema screen

- Seeing yourself through the eyes of another person

This technique works better than associated visualizations for many people. Give both approaches a go and focus on whatever gets the best results.

THE EIGHT VISUALIZATION QUESTIONS

To turbocharge the impact of the visualizations, you must make the image in your mind's eye as bright, vivid, and lifelike as possible. Turn up all the dials to the max. To do this, ask yourself the eight visualization questions:

- *Question 1*: What can I see around me?

- *Question 2*: What sounds can I hear?

- *Question 3*: What can I taste?

- *Question 4*: What can I smell?

- *Question 5*: What can I feel?

- *Question 6*: What am I thinking?

- *Question 7*: What emotions am I experiencing?

- *Question 8*: What would the person who I most admire think about me if they could see me at this moment?

For instance, picture the scenery around you, the weather, the sounds you can hear, the other people in the scene, what they are saying, the noises in the background, and so on. The more lifelike the visualization is, the better.

CHAPTER SUMMARY

In Chapter Two, I have explained various ingenious methods to help you develop the arctic-cold inner game of a dashing secret agent:

- Getting into first-class physical condition

- Using binaural beats to systematically reprogram your brain

- Revolutionizing your mental processes with cognitive behavioral therapy

- Modifying your diet to transform your mental state

- Using cutting-edge breathing and muscle relaxation techniques to obliterate stress through the mind-body connection

- Reprogramming your brain for success with autosuggestion

In Chapter Three, I will move on to reveal the secrets of an unstoppable *outer* game—the eight "persuasion weapons."

CHAPTER THREE: OUTER GAME -

ACQUIRING IRRESISTIBLE CHARM

The ability to deal with people is as purchasable a commodity as sugar or coffee, and I will pay more for that ability than for any other under the sun.

—John D Rockefeller

This chapter is all about transforming your "outer game." I will explain how to acquire scarily potent powers (known as persuasion weapons) which can exert an incredibly powerful impact on the thoughts and actions of others.

Before any respectable elite secret agent commences their mission, their handler (e.g., the debonair Q in the case of 007) makes sure they are equipped with a plethora of ingenious high-tech gadgets. This helps them successfully outwit their enemies, achieve their objectives, and return to base safely. For example, their fiendish box of technological tricks might include:

- An identification imager device. This recognizes the facial features of an individual and sends data about their characteristics to a mainframe, which then relays an in-depth profile of them back to the device

- High-powered cameras cunningly disguised as pens or buttons, which are used to take reconnaissance photos of secret documents or enemy installations

- A microchip, implanted in the agent's body, which allows mission control to track their whereabouts

- Pocket devices that can crack open safes

- Rolex wristwatches which incorporate homing beacons, lasers, or remote explosive detonators

- Special firearms with built-in optical palm readers, so that only the agent themselves can use the weapon

- A ring for the finger that emits an ultrahigh-frequency sound, which can instantly disable an enemy or shatter bulletproof glass

- A credit card which contains a versatile multiple-function lock-picking device

- A cigarette lighter packed with deadly explosives

Similarly, to effectively achieve your vital mission of becoming outrageously rich, you must have a comparable capability to outclass your enemy. I will show you powerful and proven psychological techniques to influence the minds of others, with the aim of getting them to do whatever you desire.

ITS ALL ABOUT HOW YOU SELL IT

At the risk of stating the obvious, to become wealthy (the legal way), you must persuade people to pay you money in return for providing them something of value. This could be a product (such as property, financial assets, cars, or luxury wines) or a service (such as a consulting session or investment advice). The difference between the superrich and ordinary individuals is that the superrich have the ability to either persuade many more people to pay them (e.g., Bill Gates sold Microsoft's products to a large swath of the world's population), to convince customers to pay them more (e.g., multimillionaire soccer stars get paid millions by each team they play for), or a combination of the two.

Therefore, to become rich, you will need to come up with a product or service. This could be anything, but it makes sense to choose something that plays to your strengths and life experiences.

Fortunately your product or service doesn't need to be particularly revolutionary or groundbreaking. You might be surprised to know that the amount you sell doesn't really have much to do with the quality of your product. It's usually how you *market it* that counts. In other words, how good you are at persuading others to blow the cobwebs off their wallets and part with the dough matters quite a bit.

THE PEN AND MOUTH ARE MIGHTIER THAN THE SWORD

To persuade your "target" (to use the Secret Service terminology), you must deploy a fearsome battery of scientifically based psychological techniques. I call these techniques "persuasion weapons." Getting your target to do what you want is simply a question of effectively using these powerful persuasion weapons to bypass the target's conscious thought processes and work on their subconscious mind.

As John D. Rockefeller so perceptively argues, persuasion skills are the world's most valuable commodity. We all constantly attempt to influence other people on a day-to-day basis, whether it's gaining agreement for an important business proposal, going up for a big promotion, selling or buying a product, or asking a hot girl/guy on a date. Over time, those individuals who regularly come out on top in persuasion situations will also climb to the top of the money tree too.

Every time someone communicates, they have an agenda, irrespective of whether or not they realize it on a conscious level, to persuade another person of something. Try this experiment: next time you are traveling on public transport, listen to the conversations around you. You might hear a smartly dressed business person persuading a potential customer to purchase his "must have" services, a muscle-bound tattooed thug trying to show off how damn tough he is, a charming middle-aged lady coaxing her husband to take her out to dinner that evening, a group of fashionable young guys attempting to convince everyone else in the subway of how achingly cool they are, and so on. It will soon dawn on you that, every time people open their mouths, they are engaging in persuasion of one kind or another.

159

Looking into my crystal ball for a moment, globalization and technological change mean that persuasion skills will become increasingly vital. The future belongs to those who can sell snow to the Eskimos. The rise of the Internet is creating rapidly mushrooming markets for anyone who has a decent concept to peddle and the ability to convince others to open their wallets. The most lucrative future business niches will not involve making physical products. Instead they will relate to selling ideas and to do that you need the right intellectual tool kit for becoming a persuasion grand master.

Fortunately persuasion grand masters are made and not born. The ability to influence isn't an innate talent. True expertise comes from acquiring the relevant wisdom and then consistently putting it into practice. As a famous eastern kung fu teacher once said, "Mastery comes from repetition."

Lawyers, politicians, salespeople, and con artists all practice the dark arts of using sophisticated techniques to control the behavior of others. Robert Cialdini, author of *Influence: The Psychology of Persuasion*, calls them "persuasion professionals".

Persuasion professionals take a highly methodical approach to influencing based on systematically applying certain psychological principles. Like remorseless hunters tracking down their prey, they think very shrewdly about every move they make and skillfully vary their approach, depending on the situation. Th

To discover the hidden secrets of this dastardly trade, we first need to understand the inner workings of the human mind. The world's top psychologists use something called the elaboration likelihood model (ELM)[55] to explain what makes people tick. The ELM proposes that there are two fundamental strategies of persuasion: the "central route" (System Two) and the "peripheral route" (System One). If you want to get the world dancing to your tune, you must understand how to make the best use of these two strategies, which one to apply in a particular situation, and precisely how to do so.

First let's consider the central route to persuasion. When your persuasion target is strongly interested in, and informed about, the matter at hand, the only way to sway them is with well-thought-out, logical, and coolly objective arguments. This is the central route. For example, a senior judge presiding over a high-profile murder trial would carefully weigh out all the arguments from the prosecution and the defense before deciding if to send a defendant to fry in the electric chair. This rational method of making decisions is known in the trade as System Two thinking.

---

[55] Petty, Richard E., and John T. Cacioppo. "The elaboration likelihood model of persuasion." *Advances in experimental social psychology* 19 (1986): 123-205.

People generally only operate in System Two mode when making what they regard as big decisions. The world is incredibly and increasingly fast moving and complex. There simply isn't enough time to make all (or even most) of the necessary choices required to survive and prosper using this highly logical method of thinking.

Over the course of each day, every individual will make hundreds, if not thousands, of decisions—from what shirt to wear, to whether to take the stairs or the escalator, to vitally important business judgments. If they made each of those choices based on a careful appraisal of the costs and benefits of the different alternatives, they wouldn't have time to actually do anything in life— it would be a case of "analysis paralysis". For this reason, people do not generally use the rational, logical System Two approach that the murder trial judge adopts.

This brings us to the peripheral route to persuasion. People generally operate on autopilot, making spur-of-the-moment snap judgments about what to do based on animal instinct and intuition. This is known as System One thinking. System One involves reflexive, subconscious, and automatic decisions.

System One thinking derives from certain evolutionarily hardwired "rules of thumb." These simple rules allow humans to survive in the modern world by providing a time-efficient response in situations where a decision is not worth focusing on, either because it is relatively trivial or just too complicated.

The existence of these wired-in behavioral rules is a rather mixed blessing. They work well for the decision maker, for the most part, in terms of preventing valuable time from being wasted on pondering trifling or unsolvable issues. However, devious persuasion professionals can use the peripheral route to systematically exploit their target's habitual reliance on System One thinking to their own advantage.

I am going to explain how to use peripheral-route-based persuasion to powerfully influence others, using communication operating on the automatic, subconscious System One level.

COMPUTERS, ELEPHANTS, AND RIDERS

In the previous chapter on autosuggestion, I explained that you should consider the brain being like a computer. This analogy also helps explain the variance between System One and System Two thinking.

A computer can multitask, meaning it can run several different programs at once. You can see some programs running on the computer screen, such as Internet Explorer or Microsoft Office. These visible programs are equivalent to your *conscious* brain (System Two thinking). However, there are also numerous other programs quietly running in the background, which you are generally blissfully unaware of. These software packages are like your *unconscious* brain (System One thinking). There is more to your mind than simply the visible part that relates to your conscious thought.

Another way to think of the brain is as an elephant and a human rider making their merry way through a humid tropical jungle[56]. The rider represents the rational, deliberative, conscious brain (System Two thinking) while the elephant represents the automatic, subconscious brain (System One thinking).

So, who determines the course that they will collectively take through the jungle? Who decides whether they go left or right as they reach each juncture? Is it the intrepid rider or the ponderous elephant? Well, since the rider is sitting astride the elephant and holding the reins, he appears to be the one calling the shots. However, as the rider is relatively small in stature compared to the elephant, he is often unable to control the larger animal. Sometimes the elephant just does his own thing and cheerfully sets off in a seemingly random direction. The elephant regularly navigates his own path through the forest, responding automatically, unconsciously, and instinctively to the

---

[56] Vaisey, Stephen. "Motivation and Justification: A Dual-Process Model of Culture in Action1." *American Journal of Sociology* 114, no. 6 (2009): 1675-1715.

environment around him, much to the intense frustration of the rider.

The human brain works in exactly the same way. Sometimes the reasonable, conscious mind is holding the rudder and rationally charts the optimal course through life. Nonetheless, for the majority of the time, the unconscious brain (System One) is actually making the decisions.

You are probably painfully familiar with situations where you have stuffed yourself with too much food, tried and failed miserably to quit smoking or drinking, or generally acted like a lazy goat, despite your best intentions. This is the unconscious brain taking precedence over the conscious brain.

Often the conscious brain mistakenly thinks it is in charge, even though it isn't. Actually the subconscious is in the driving seat. The conscious brain then simply justifies that decision after it has been made. In other words, the conscious mind thinks it is the CEO when it is really just the director of communications.

For example, you might determine, on a subconscious level, to stuff yourself with a huge spicy lamb kebab with double fries and extra chili sauce. The conscious brain justifies this gross overconsumption by thinking *I can start my strict new diet next week, so it's fine to indulge a little on this occasion*. Situations where you pathetically cave in and display a pitiful lack of willpower are usually due to your subconscious mind dominating your conscious thought.

Therefore, the fact that the brain operates like the elephant and the rider implies that the secret to persuading others is often to speak directly to their unsuspecting subconscious elephant (System One) brain rather than their rational (System Two) rider brain.

THE EIGHT DEADLY WEAPONS OF PERSUASION

Next, I will explain the eight deadly weapons of persuasion, which are all based on the peripheral route and therefore, manipulate the System One brain. As you wield these weapons with increasing skill, you can easily trigger automatic psychological responses in your persuasion targets, influencing them to respond to your wishes on an involuntary level.

For each of the weapons, I give examples on how they can be applied. These examples are illustrative rather than exhaustive, and you can also use your creative abilities to think of your own techniques to apply the weapons.

The eight deadly weapons (which you can remember using the acronym which conveniently spells out the two words "My Weapon"—see text in table below, under Persuasion Weapon column) are as follows:

Section	Persuasion Weapon	Fundamental Principle
A	Persuasion Weapon One: **M**anipulating by priming	*Your target is the rat, and you control the laboratory*
B	Persuasion Weapon Two: **Y**ou're looking good	*Look smoking hot to leverage the "halo effect"*
C	Persuasion Weapon Three: **W**earing the crown of authority	*Everybody follows the "leader," so look like the goddamn leader*
D	Persuasion Weapon Four: **E**xtending the hand of friendship	*You have to make friends to influence people*
E	Persuasion Weapon Five: **A**ccessing the subconscious mind	*Use hypnotic language patterns to bypass the gatekeeper and speak directly with the subconscious mind*
F	Persuasion Weapon Six: **P**roving popularity	*Most targets are sheep, so tell them which direction the herd is going in*
G	Persuasion Weapon Seven: **O**bligating to gain commitment	*A gentleman's word is his bond*
H	Persuasion Weapon Eight: **N**udging using incentives	*Dangle the carrot and wield the stick*

A PERSUASION WEAPON NUMBER ONE: MANIPULATING BY PRIMING

The greatest con that humanity ever fell for is the lie that people control their own brains. Most individuals assume that they have free will. In other words, they believe that each time they engage in a particular activity—whether it's speaking to friends, working, eating and drinking, daydreaming, playing with their children, buying and selling, and so on—that they are doing so on the basis of a deliberate, conscious choice.

However, this is actually a universal misperception. Often, just like unsuspecting rats in a laboratory experiment, humans make decisions on an instinctive basis in response to stimuli (sights, sounds, smells, tastes, and textures) in their immediate environment. Afterward their conscious mind then *convinces* them that they have actually made the choice freely based on a deliberate, logical thought process. In fact the famous behavioral psychologist B. F. Skinner argued that all free will is an illusion.

Priming is a powerful psychological technique which acts directly on the hidden depths of the target's subliminal mind. Priming is often seen as a very controversial and manipulative method because it acts outside conscious awareness. Unscrupulous operators can use it to make individuals "act against their own will."

Priming involves exposing your target to a stimulus *before* they make a decision in a deliberate attempt to alter their subconscious thinking and therefore their behavior. Priming stimuli can take the form of sights, sounds, smells, or sensations.

Businesses often use the devilishly clever priming technique to turboboost their sales. For example, grocery stores vary the music that they play at different times of the week to shrewdly prime naive customers into modifying their purchasing behavior.

Most people visit the grocery store on Saturday morning for their weekly shopping and typically throw the same products in the basket every time. They stick to a standard shopping list, which doesn't change much from one trip to the next. The smart grocery retailer wants to get shoppers to whiz around the aisles and get to the checkout with their weekly purchase; to make space in the shop for other paying customers. So they belt out fast tempo music (e.g., pop, rock, or electronic dance music) to make their patrons to dash around the store.

But on Sunday, when the wily grocer has fewer customers, he plays a different game. Sunday shoppers are something of a different breed. They are usually more relaxed and more open-minded about trying new products, such as an unfamiliar variety of cheese, meat, or bread. Therefore, on Sunday, it is profitable for stores to coax their clientele to take a more leisurely stroll around the store so that they squander more of their hard-earned cash on novel and exotic purchases. They do this by treating their customers to the soothing sounds and mellow harmonies of classical music or jazz.

Note that this cynical musical manipulation does not influence behavior on a *conscious* level. Shoppers do not think *Ah, I can hear the tranquil sound of Beethoven, so I should slow down a bit and consider purchasing some gluten-free organic Mongolian goat's cheese.* Instead, providing a musical stimulus *subconsciously* primes shoppers to change their purchasing behavior.

Scientists have conducted mountains of research that show just how scarily powerful priming really is:

- One study primed a group of people with words associated with decrepit old age, such as "forgetful" and "wrinkle." A similar group of people were primed with a neutral stimulus (words without any particular connotation). The researchers then measured the speed at which the participants exited the testing area at the end of the study. Even though the researchers did not explicitly mention speed or slowness, the group who were primed with the elderly stereotype walked out of the room much more slowly.[57]

- Another study primed one group of people with rude and naughty words, another group with nice, polite words, and a third group with neutral words. The researchers found that the group primed with the profanities was more likely to interrupt the interviewer than those primed with the neutral words. Conversely the group primed with the polite words was more likely to keep quiet.[58]

- Restaurants exude a distinct and edifying aroma that is very noticeable to passersby in the near vicinity. This acts wonderfully as a prime for hunger. Many grocery stores use the smell of baked bread in a similarly enticing way.

- Evidence shows that strategically placing fitness-inspiring objects, such as sports magazines and sports

---

57 Dijksterhuis, S., J. Bargh, "The Perception-Behaviour Expressway: Automatic Effects of Social Perception on Social Behaviour," edited by In Zanna, *Advances in Experimental Social Psychology* 33 (2001): 1–40.
58 Bargh, J., M. Chen, L. Burrows, "Automaticity of Social Behavior: Direct Effects of Trait Construct and Stereotype Activation on Action," *Journal of Personality and Social Psychology* 71(2) (1996): 230–44.

shoes in a certain area, can prime healthy behavior, such as undertaking vigorous exercise.[59]

- A study showed that priming can improve an individual's ability to achieve complicated tasks. Researchers asked one group of people to imagine a scholarly university professor so they could prime them with the concept of "intelligence." They asked a similar group of people to imagine riotous and thuggish football hooligans to prime them for "stupidity." The group who were primed to think about the academics performed significantly better on subsequent general knowledge tests than the other group.[60]

Here are a few other examples of how priming can be used effectively to make money:

- An ingenious real estate agent who I know systematically primes his customers with the concept of wealth each time he markets a property. For instance, he ostentatiously parks his upmarket Jaguar in the

---

59 Wryobeck, J., M. Chen, "Using Priming Techniques to Facilitate Health Behaviours," *Clinical Psychologist* 7 (2003): 105–108.
60 Dijksterhuis, W., W. Knippenberg, "The Relation Between Perception and Behaviour or How to Win a Game of Trivial Pursuit," *Journal of Personality and Social Psychology* 74(4) (1998): 865–877.

driveway, leaves smart yachting and fashion magazines casually scattered across the coffee table, and artfully positions a bottle of exquisite champagne in an ice bucket in the kitchen. These little touches let him charge a massive markup and obtain enormous profits.

- A comedian friend primes his audience to find his set amusing by asking them all to take a pen out of their pockets or handbags and clench it between their teeth. Top psychologist Daniel Kahneman explains that putting a pen in your mouth horizontally forces you to smile, which makes you feel happier as a consequence, and more receptive to humor[61]. Therefore this simple trick makes the audience find my friend's jokes funnier and ensures that he gets rebooked.

- An acquaintance of mine runs an advertising company. He knows that he needs to harness the full creative impulses of his employees to maximize his profits. Therefore he systematically primes his workers for creativity. He plays eclectic and exotic music in the office, orders unusual international cuisine for lunch, adorns his office space with avant garde artwork and sculptures, and awards artistic sounding job titles such

---

[61] Kahneman, D. *'Thinking Fast and Slow'* (2011) p54

as Chief Troublemaker, Digital Prophet and Ambassador of Buzz. This might sound goofy but his track record at beating his competitors speaks for itself.

Example: Systematically prime your target. The basic principle is to consider which primes you can expose your target to in their immediate environment shortly before they make a crunch decision. You are the all-powerful scientist; the target is the unaware experimental rat, and your environment is the controlled laboratory. Consider how you can modify what they see, hear, smell, feel, and taste in order to prime the desired behavior.

B PERSUASION WEAPON NUMBER TWO: YOU'RE LOOKING GOOD

The old saying claims that "You can't judge a book by its cover," but, in reality, most people do just that.

Megapowerful and wealthy multinational corporations invest untold squillions of dollars in TV advertisements with the sole aim of persuading the dumb masses to part with their hard-earned cash. Just ask yourself this one simple question: do these ads ever feature actors who look like they have fallen out of the ugly tree and hit every branch on the way down? No. The companies pay through the nose to feature the world's most breathtakingly beautiful people in their commercials. Does having a sizzling hot female ingenue in your promo actually make your product of an inherently higher quality? Hell no, but it sure gets your merchandise flying off the shelves!

Similarly consider how the top salespeople in successful companies look and dress. Do you ever see someone with a face as ugly as a smashed pie, a profoundly unflattering haircut, a terrible body odor problem, and disheveled and stained clothing showing high-rolling VIP customers the latest Lamborghini? No, they are usually tightly buttocked, perfectly groomed, and immaculately dressed. Does the latter type person necessarily possess more knowledge about automobiles than the former? No, but you can bet your bottom dollar that they move more luxury vehicles off the lot!

Although it may seem rather unfair, physical attractiveness has a dramatic impact on your ability to influence. This is because of a ubiquitous psychological phenomenon known as the "halo effect." Individuals habitually and irrationally extend favorable impressions about particular traits to other completely unconnected traits[62].

On one hand, the superficial public tends to groundlessly assume that those who possess dazzling looks are more intelligent, kind, honest, and enjoy a whole host of other admirable characteristics. On the other hand, those who are not so easy on the eye are often unjustly assumed to be dishonest, stupid, and weak-minded. Actually scientists have found no evidence of a relationship between brainpower and "babepower," but this does not prevent the halo effect from working its peculiar magic.

The halo effect exerts a shockingly strong influence on people's behavior. For example, handsome candidates received more

---

[62] Nisbett, Richard E., and Timothy D. Wilson. "The halo effect: Evidence for unconscious alteration of judgments." *Journal of personality and social psychology* 35, no. 4 (1977): 250.

than 2.5 times as many votes in the 1974 Canadian federal elections over ugly candidates. This is despite the fact that most voters adamantly denied that the physical attractiveness of candidates had any influence on their decision whatsoever[63]. In summary, if you wish to become a persuasion grand master, it is imperative that you look your best at all times.

- *Example: Get into shape.* Follow the training program in Section A of Chapter 1 to whip yourself into superb shape and turboboost your influencing skills.

- *Example: Dress fashionably.* Make a habit of keeping on top of the latest fashions. If you dress twice as well as the person standing next to you then this should allow you to persuade twice as effectively too.

---

[63] Cialdini, Robert B. "Compliance principles of compliance professionals: Psychologists of necessity." In *Social Influence: The Ontario Symposium,* vol. 5, pp. 165-184. Lawrence Erlbaum Associates Hillsdale, NJ, 1987.

C PERSUASION WEAPON NUMBER THREE: WEARING THE CROWN OF AUTHORITY

I once had a neighbor who was a hardened chain smoker, puffing and wheezing his way through one hundred "cancer sticks" a day. His fingers were a revolting shade of nicotine-stained yellow, his breath stunk like a filthy old ashtray, his teeth looked like decaying tombstones, and he ran out of breath climbing the stairs.

His wife and kids had begged him to quit for literally decades. They knew his foul habit was slowly poisoning him, and they naturally wanted the foolish bugger to live to a ripe old age. Even his best drinking buddies started to drop hints that he might not dodge his coffin for too much longer if he kept cruelly abusing his own lungs, but it was to no avail. None of them could convince him to stop lighting up. It was like talking to a brick wall.

However, one day his kindly doctor lost his patience and gave him a candid and stern talking to about his smoking, going into lurid and graphic detail about the serious damage he was inflicting upon his health. My neighbor was profoundly shaken by his physician's advice and made a heartfelt resolution to never put a cigarette to his lips again. Fifteen years later, he is still a proud nonsmoker.

So how could a doctor persuade him to quit so easily when his caring and loving family had failed so miserably? The simple reason is the psychological principle of *authority*. In a complex and sometimes dangerous world, we automatically turn to experts to tell us what to do. The power of authority can be so great that, even in a life-or-death situation, the majority of people will defer to an expert's view over the advice of family and friends, or even their own common sense.

The reason that people place such blind faith in a man of medicine is because of their familiar trappings of authority. This includes their title, bedside manner, white coat, stethoscope around the neck, and so on. These accoutrements serve as a strong signal that "this guy knows what he is talking about."

Of course, other professions which have authority, such as hotshot entrepreneurs, corporate chieftains, big-league politicians, police bigwigs, and so on, all unmistakably project a comparable sort of "expert power."[64]

Here is the rub. Although the natural human tendency to defer to authority can undoubtedly have benefits in certain situations, you can also take advantage of this predisposition to help persuade a target to do your every bidding.

---

[64] Kelman, HC. *Crimes of obedience: Toward a social psychology of authority and responsibility* (1989)

A first-rate example where authority is employed manipulatively is the widespread use of celebrities to promote products. A renowned sportsperson or famous actor is no more likely than the next guy on the street to have a special knowledge of watches or perfume, but their endorsement of a particular brand of these products is like gold dust in advertising terms.

Canny advertising executives often use an actor's well-known screen persona to cunningly imply that the thespian has corresponding expert knowledge relating to that role. For example, an actor who is famous for playing a doctor on television may appear in a white coat and endorse a company's drug or health product. Even though the celebrity is in all likelihood sublimely ignorant of the product he is promoting, his endorsement still gets the cash registers ringing[65].

You can easily *create an impression* of authority to persuade your target, even when you are, in fact, just a run-of-the-mill dude. Here are some deliberate cues that you can employ to "remind your target who is in charge," making them more likely to do what you want.

---

[65] Erdogan, B. Zafer. "Celebrity endorsement: A literature review." *Journal of marketing management* 15, no. 4 (1999): 291-314.

PILE ON THE "BLING"

If you wish to create an undisputable impression of authority, then you must "speculate to accumulate" and invest prudently in status symbols which are congruent with this "personal brand"[66]:

- *Example: Look the part.* Generally speaking, a well-fitted tailored suit is a must. Expensive-looking shoes are de rigueur. Watches and phones are brightly flashing status indicators, so make sure that you sport high-quality makes. Other potent power signals include keys to a high-status luxury car and terribly expensive-looking cigar boxes.

- *Example: Dress like an insider.* There are "in" clothes and "out" clothes in any context. To create an authoritative impression, you must consistently dress in the "in" clothes. A friend of mine who works as a trader for a London investment bank told me an amusing story about how all his ambitious colleagues copy their bosses' dressing style, right down to the type of cuff links and socks they wear, in a shameless attempt to climb

---

[66] Goffman, Erving. "Symbols of class status." *The British Journal of Sociology* 2, no. 4 (1951): 294-304.

the greasy career ladder. So swallow your pride, stifle your originality, look at how the "movers and shakers" in your environment dress, and brazenly copy them.

HAVE MORE TITLES THAN AN AFRICAN DICTATOR

Prestigious designations convey authority. Educational titles such as doctor or professor, organizational titles such as director or chief executive, or aristocratic titles, such as lord or duke, make it as clear as day that their bearer is high up on the social totem pole[67]:

- *Example: Acquire a high-status title.* For instance, if you own a company, however small, then award yourself a grand high-falutin' title, such as president, chairman, or something similar.

- You can also easily purchase "degrees" and "PhDs" from online universities for a few hundred dollars. These "esteemed" qualifications are awarded on the basis of "life experience," which you can conveniently prove

---

[67] Bourdieu, Pierre. "The social space and the genesis of groups." *Theory and society* 14, no. 6 (1985): 723-744.

through submitting a short and perfunctory essay.

- If you have a bit more moolah, it is also possible to buy lordships online for a perfectly reasonable contribution.

- *Example: Promote your title wherever possible.* Ensure that you always introduce yourself using your correct designation. If you initially feel self-conscious about doing so, then use a written introduction first or ask other people to "accidentally" mention your title.

- Display evidence of your respected qualifications as prominently as possible in your immediate vicinity to prove your intellectual caliber. This could include framed certificates or graduation photographs proving achievement of PhDs, professional qualifications, and so on.

- You can also legally change your own name to make yourself sound more "old money." So if you're a plain old "John Smith" or "Lee Taylor," then change to something more high society, such as Crispian Roxton-Quimby.

STRUT LIKE A PEACOCK

Fake it until you make it. If you act like you're the big enchilada, then most people will bow to your implied superiority on the off chance you are actually someone of great import. Start from the assumption that you rule the roost, and your supine targets should become like putty in your hands[68].

- *Example: Put yourself on a pedestal.* Always act as if you are on a higher (professional/social/sexual) status level than you actually are. For example, if you own a small software start-up, then behave like you are Steve Jobs. If you own a microbrewery, then carry yourself like the head of the Guinness family.

TALK THE TALK

I have just told you that in any social setting there are "in" clothes and "out" clothes. Well, there is also "in" language and "out" language. If you want to become the head honcho, you need to know the lingo. Every profession—from lawyers and bankers to drug dealers, pimps, and fraudsters—has its own jargon, and

---

[68] Snyder, Mark, Elizabeth D. Tanke, and Ellen Berscheid. "Social perception and interpersonal behavior: On the self-fulfilling nature of social stereotypes." *Journal of Personality and Social Psychology* 35, no. 9 (1977): 656.

this separates those "in the know" from those who aren't. [69] Again, what constitutes "in" language varies with context, so listen to the main players and flexibly tailor your language to the situation.

- *Example: Speak fluent "in" language.* Copy how the movers and shakers in your social circle communicate to learn how to speak the "in" language.

HANG OUT WITH THE IN-CROWD

Birds of a feather flock together. High-status individuals mix in high-status circles, while losers attract fellow losers. If you cultivate the impression of being extraordinarily well-networked, or acting on behalf of the big fish in the pond, then the magic of their authority must surely rub off on you as well[70].

- *Example: Elbow your way into the circles of power.* Use

---

[69] Nash, Jeffrey E., Darwin L. Thomas, and Andrew J. Weigert. "Code elaboration and self-concept states." *The Journal of social psychology* 90, no. 1 (1973): 45-51.

[70] Cialdini, Robert B., and Maralou E. De Nicholas. "Self-presentation by association." *Journal of personality and social psychology* 57, no. 4 (1989): 626.

any excuse to forge connections with high-status people. Find out what topics are on their minds so you can easily strike up and hold a mutually beneficial conversation with them. When others see you socializing with the top dogs, they are likely to classify you in the same social bracket.

- *Example: Name drop.* Use first names to refer to high-status people so that it looks like you are old buddies who go back a long way. For example, refer to Queen Elizabeth as "Old Liz" or Bill Gates as "Billy." This is a well-established technique, but it still works like a charm.

MAKE YOURSELF (AND YOUR PRODUCT) SCARCE

As is well known by accomplished flirts all over the world, people want what they can't have. This understanding underpins the time-honored romantic strategy of "playing hard to get." If someone is found to be "easy", then your desire for them diminishes, while love which must be hard-won inflames the passions.

The same principle applies in other areas of life, such as

business. If you restrict the supply of something or, in other words, make it scarce, then your target should lust after it. [71]

- *Example: Use common sales ruses,* like "buy while stocks last," "limited number in stock," and "closing-down sale" to make your products seem scarce and therefore as valuable as pure platinum.

- *Example: Limit your affection.* Sometimes you can make the schoolboy error of showering those whom you are attracted to with attention in an ungainly attempt to win their hearts. But unfortunately this pitiful overavailability identifies you as a worthless deadbeat. Strictly ration your affections to get their pulses racing.

- *Example: Increase the perceived value of your time.* To look like someone with important places to go and people to see, do the following:

    - Buzz around like a blue-assed fly. Walk quickly and with a sense of unwavering purpose, like someone on a vital mission.

---

[71] Lynn, Michael. "Scarcity effects on value: A quantitative review of the commodity theory literature." *Psychology & Marketing* 8, no. 1 (1991): 43-57.

- Give the impression of a jam-packed schedule. If a target wants to meet with you, imply that you only have very limited time slots free to see them—e.g., "I might have an available slot in three weeks on Thursday from 8:30 a.m. to 9:00 a.m."

- Say things like, "I can't stay and chat for long. I only have a few minutes," or politely disengage from conversations after a reasonable amount of time, to imply that "you have places to be."

- *Example: Show the buyer the competition.* This works because, like the lady choosing between two suitors, rivalry has the effect of powerfully increasing desire for whomever, or whatever, is being vied for. For instance, real estate agents often invite all the potential buyers to view a property at the same time, rather than one after another. This can provoke the buyers into a ferocious, no-holds-barred bidding war, driving up prices and profits.

D PERSUASION WEAPON NUMBER FOUR: EXTENDING THE HAND OF FRIENDSHIP

Apparently nice guys finish last, but when it comes to the science of persuasion, this statement is about as false as it gets. In reality the firm hand of friendship will usually drag you over the finish line in first place.

The most monstrous of adversaries will often melt like soft butter when confronted with a friendly, smiling face. The Viking warriors of the 8th to 11th century were infamous for invading sleepy coastal villages like a plague of malevolent locusts, laying waste to everything in their hairy, sweaty paths. If a hapless peasant so much as muttered a mild objection, he would get a thorough "working over" by the brutish Nordic invaders. Many a "hero" regretted their bravery while forlornly picking up their broken teeth off the floor.

However, the notorious Vikings had a highly rigid code of honor. Anybody who showed the appropriate amount of respect and a sense of humor was generally spared and even invited to join in their debauched revelry (gulp!). If being pleasant won the day with despised and feared Vikings, it will work with just about anyone, so sit tight, and I will teach you How to be Nice 101.

SMILE AND THE WORLD WILL SMILE BACK

The first rule of acting nice is to approach the target with a beaming smile plastered all over your ugly mug. A relaxed smile indicates friendly intentions. Let's face it. The world today is literally teeming with stir-crazy psychos, especially in grimy, danger-ridden metropolises like New York or London. When you strike up a conversation with a target, the first thing to cross their mind is normally "Am I in danger?" If their alarm bells start ringing, then they will bail out and terminate the dialogue, but, if you smile, their guard will drop instantly.

Smiling also conveys the laid-back confidence of a hassle-free and successful man-or-woman-about-town. Numerous scientific studies have shown that high-status people smile much more than the average person, so smiling makes you look more important too[72].

Relaxed body language goes hand in hand with smiling in creating an impression of sincere and helpful friendliness. Have you ever come across someone who, although they say all the right things, somehow makes your skin crawl? This is usually

---

[72] Kraut, Robert E., and Robert E. Johnston. "Social and emotional messages of smiling: An ethological approach." *Journal of personality and social psychology* 37, no. 9 (1979): 1539.

because they are signaling their evil intentions through nonverbal leakage or body language; which is disturbingly inconsistent with their verbal communication. If you are making friendly noises but indicating ignoble motives with the rest of your body, then the target will believe their eyes rather than their ears. To persuade effectively, your body language must be transmitting a congruent message[73].

- *Example:* Smile!

- *Example:* Use relaxed body language. This includes the following:

    - Open arms and legs (so the torso and groin area are exposed). Obviously, if you are wearing a skirt, then don't do this.

    - Making casual eye contact

    - Hands relaxed and "making shapes" to illustrate and emphasize points made

    - Full and easy smile

---

[73] Borg, James. *Body language: 7 easy lessons to master the silent language.* (2009).

- Clear speech (no muttering or mumbling)

LET THE LOVE SHINE FROM WITHIN YOU

What goes around comes around. Targets are more disposed to like people who like *them* in return. Psychologists understand that this is a completely natural reaction. Once your target knows that you think highly of them, they are psychologically compelled to look for things that they like about you too[74]. Their subconscious reasoning is *I know that I am a great person. If this other guy likes me, he must be a pretty good egg as well.*

Example: Think the best of your target. Work up a feeling of sincere and passionate admiration for your target, and your love for them will shine through in your body language. They should be powerless to resist reciprocating your affections and therefore hang on your every word like a starstruck groupie.

To make your body language literally radiate adoration, think of at least one thing that you really admire about the target. Even someone like Attila the Hun probably had a good side, right?

---

[74] Kenny, David A., and Lawrence La Voie. "Reciprocity of interpersonal attraction: A confirmed hypothesis." *Social Psychology Quarterly* (1982): 54-58.

Mentally focus on, and compliment them on, that positive characteristic before, and while, interacting with them. Think the world of your target and your persuasion hit rate will skyrocket.

BE LIKE A BAD PENNY - ALWAYS TURNING UP

Does "familiarity breed contempt"? Apparently not, as top psychologists claim that this old cliché gets reality completely backward. Actually familiarity breeds *liking*. The more time we spend with someone, the more we ought to grow on them[75].

This is why people are often firm friends with their weird neighbors and work colleagues, even when they have less in common than Mother Teresa and Jimi Hendrix.

---

[75] Newcomb, Theodore M. "The prediction of interpersonal attraction." *American psychologist* 11, no. 11 (1956): 575.

The more frequently we interact with someone, the stronger that bond of friendship should form. So, if you want a target to eat out of your hand, then make sure that you are never out of their sight.

- *Example: Become familiar to maximize your chances of successful persuasion.*

BECOME YOUR TARGET'S DOPPELGÄNGER

In German folklore, a doppelgänger is a look-alike or double of a living person. We are drawn to, and are more likely to do the wishes of, those who are similar to us. Therefore, to get your target to do what you want, you should become their doppelgänger and faithfully copy everything about them.

Birds of a feather flock together. We prefer those who are a mirror image of ourselves. Admittedly we may find dissimilar people exotically charming for a while, hence the phrase "opposites attract." But ultimately we tend to form emotional bonds with other people on the basis of what we have in common. Our psychological processes haven't really evolved since the days of our prehistoric tribal ancestors. We are hardwired to see "similar" as "friend," and "different" as "foe."[76] Even in this day and age we still sort ourselves into tribal groups based on perceived similarities.

The irresistible power of rapport is common knowledge among persuasion professionals. Salespeople are systematically trained to sniff out, or even invent, common interests with prospective buyers. They are taught to ingratiate themselves with customers through saying things like "I noticed your Irish accent. I am originally from Ireland myself," or "I see that you are wearing an Iron Maiden T-shirt. I am a huge fan of that band too." They know very well that building rapport is the key to a big fat sales commission.

- *Example: Systematically match the body language and posture of your target.* This is known as mirroring; acting as if you are a looking glass for your target's nonverbal communication. For instance, if the target leans forward, then you lean forward. If they then lean back, you lean back. If they cross their arms, then cross yours too.

- Also discretely imitate the target's speech patterns in terms of their tone, inflection, tempo, and volume. For example, if they speak quickly and excitedly, then copy

---

[76] Byrne, Donn. "Interpersonal attraction and attitude similarity." *The Journal of Abnormal and Social Psychology* 62, no. 3 (1961): 713.

this. If they talk loudly, then raise your own voice. If they have a distinct accent, then try to speak with a broadly similar twang. However take care not to mirror your target in an *overly* obvious fashion. They might get wise to your game, suspect manipulation, and respond negatively.

- *Example: Take an interest in your target's life and pursuits.* You might be surprised to know that becoming a persuasion maestro isn't really about being a silver-tongued smooth talker and dazzling your audience with your erudite wit, like a modern day Oscar Wilde.

- The real secret to creating unbreakable rapport with your target is to provide them a platform to enjoy the pleasantly ego-boosting activity of talking about *themselves*. At the risk of repeating the platitudinous advice doled out in women's magazines, everybody loves a great listener!

- Remember that to be fascinating you must be *fascinated*. Talk for no more than 20 percent of the conversation. Let the target happily waffle away for the other 80 percent. Be more enthralled by them and their life than anyone has been before. The more utterly captivated you are by them, the more they will warm to you, establishing a good rapport.

- *Example: To effectively influence your target, first find out their opinions on life-or-death matters such as politics, religion, and football, and then shamelessly agree with them.* The quickest way to shatter a relationship is to attack their fundamentally held views.

- *Example: Tune in to the same emotional wavelength as your target.* If you can lay on the empathy with a whoppingly great shovel, then they must surely open up like a blossoming flower.

- Empathizing essentially involves first doing a bit of careful sleuthing to identify the things that are playing on your target's mind. Afterward, demonstrate that either you are currently "in the same boat," or at least that you have been previously. For example, imagine that the target is feeling downhearted because he has just split up with an evil bitch of a wife. In this case, you should explain that you have previously had your heart cruelly broken too. This will show that you know what it's like to "walk a mile in his shoes." The more fellowship you can show, the better. Be completely "in the moment" as your target reveals their deepest desires to you. Really and truly care about them, and you should be repaid tenfold.

- *Example: Remember your target's name.* One of the best methods to create rapport is to give the target the basic respect of remembering their name.

- Let me tell you about a famous technique used by the great French leader Napoleon. Every time you are introduced to a new acquaintance, make a mental note of their name. As soon as you get the opportunity, grab a paper and pen, and scribble it down for future reference. This makes sure you remember what they are called and thus helps you forge a potentially valuable friendship.

GIVE YOUR TARGET A WARM, FUZZY GLOW

We are inexorably drawn, like moths to a flame, toward those who make us feel happy, appreciated, and important. To become a veritable persuasion champion, make sure that you "always look on the bright side," genuinely complimenting your targets on their good points and singing their praises to others[77].

- *Example: Be the life and soul of the party.* Make yourself more likable through creating a lighthearted, friendly, and humorous demeanor.

- *Example: Blow your target's trumpet.* Targets adore

---

[77] Lieberman, David J. *Get Anyone to Do Anything: Never Feel Powerless Again--With Psychological Secrets to Control and Influence Every Situation* (2010)

compliments, so reveal to them the depths of your undying admiration. Dale Carnegie expressed this principle very eloquently when he stated that "The unvarnished truth is that almost all the people you meet feel themselves superior to you in some way, and a sure way to their hearts is to let them realize, in some subtle way, that you recognize their importance and recognize it sincerely."

- Identify something praiseworthy about the target and sincerely compliment this feature of theirs. For instance, if they have an attractive smile, then draw attention to it. If they are wearing rather elegant shoes, then say as much. If they have a cheery and agreeable personality, then say how much you like it. The more loved and lovely you can make them feel, the easier you can steer them in the desired direction. As Abraham Lincoln bluntly opined, "Everyone likes a compliment."

- *Example: Don't be negative.* The other side of the coin to flattery getting you everywhere is that criticism will go down like a lead balloon with a big fat elephant tied to it. Therefore, strenuously avoid giving criticism whenever possible; it is a surefire way of making a mortal enemy for life. Avoid getting into arguments. Even if you know you are firmly in the right, it is often wiser to neatly sidestep an argument because of the danger that you will wound the target's brittle self-esteem when you prove them wrong. Sometimes it's better to lose the battle so that you can win the war of maintaining first-rate and profitable relationships.

- *Example: Be your target's greatest cheerleader.* Never fail to sing your target's praises to others. Your zealous admiration will eventually find its way back to them, making the flowers of friendship blossom gorgeously

- Actually psychological studies have shown that "secondhand praise" of this kind is *more* credible and effective than direct compliments. It is seen as more sincere and genuine then brazenly flattering someone to their face[78].

---

[78] Lieberman, David J. *Get Anyone to Do Anything: Never Feel Powerless Again--With Psychological Secrets to Control and Influence Every Situation* (2010).

DON'T BE THE MESSENGER THAT GETS SHOT

Strive to be the bearer of good rather than bad tidings. It is a well-known psychological law that when you combine yourself with a *positive* stimulus your target is likely to eventually associate you with that stimulus. For instance, when enjoying a lovely holiday, you often attribute the pleasant "holiday feeling" to those people around you at the time. This is why so many highly dubious holiday romances flourish[79].

It also works the other way around too. If you inadvertently habitually combine yourself with *negative* stimuli, then the target will eventually feel a sense of heavy gloom every time he casts eyes on you.

For instance, hapless office workers with the unfortunate task of regularly relaying poor organizational performance data to their executive board are destined to become hated. This is true even if the underperformance is in no way their fault. The unlucky messenger usually does get the proverbial bellyful of lead.

- *Example: Always associate yourself with good news rather than bad news.*

---

[79] Ibid

GET OUT YOUR BEGGAR'S TIN CUP TO GET POPULAR

You might think that making a habit of asking for favors would make you about as popular as an angry wasp at a family picnic. But, perhaps counterintuitively to some, asking for help generally brings out people's warm, fuzzy, and altruistic side, to aid you in getting what you want.

This phenomenon is named the Benjamin Frankin Effect after the famous Founding Father of the United States. Franklin explains how he got a rival politician onside whilst serving in the Pennsylvania legislature in the 18th century: "Having heard that he had in his library a certain very scarce and curious book, I wrote a note to him, expressing my desire of perusing that book, and requesting he would do me the favour of lending it to me for a few days. He sent it immediately, and I return'd it in about a week with another note, expressing strongly my sense of the favour. When we next met in the House, he spoke to me (which he had never done before), and with great civility; and he ever after manifested a readiness to serve me on all occasions".[80]

---

[80] J. A. Leo Lemay & P. M. Zall, eds., *Benjamin Franklin's Autobiography: A Norton Critical Edition* (1986).

The Benjamin Frankin Effect works because of the handy psychological principle of cognitive dissonance. When we do someone a good turn, our mind naturally questions why we wasted our valuable time doing this rather than sensibly looking out for number one. This creates a rather unpleasant sensation of psychological tension known as cognitive dissonance. To get rid of this ghastly feeling, we rationalize that we must have made such an effort at helping them *because we like them*. Otherwise, why did we do it, right? And once we start thinking fondly about someone, as we have already established, we become dangerously vulnerable to manipulation. Therefore, asking for favors is a fiendishly clever method of turboboosting your persuasion powers[81].

- *Example: Look for opportunities to ask targets for small favors.*

---

[81] Schopler, J; Compere, J.S. (1971). "Effects of being kind or harsh to another on liking.". *Journal of Personality and Social Psychology* **20** (2): 155–159

ONE GOOD TURN DESERVES ANOTHER
(BIGGER ONE)

In a nutshell, the principle of reciprocity is essentially: If I scratch your back, then you should scratch mine. If I do something for you now, then you will probably feel obliged to return the favor and do something for me later.

Evolutionary biology explains that reciprocal behavior developed in humans because it helps build the cooperative relationships essential for survival. If I save *you* from the gruesome fate of being mauled to death by a woolly mammoth, then you would commonly feel obliged to leap to my defense the next time *my* life is in deadly peril. The desire to reciprocate helps inspire people to work together effectively as a team, increasing the likelihood that they will live long enough to pass on their genes. A belligerent mammoth would fancy its chances against a solitary human, but against a determined group working in cahoots; it hasn't got a chance in hell. Reciprocity is the glue that holds society together, because it makes long-term, mutually beneficial relationships both desirable and possible.

However, a target's desire to reciprocate acts can leave them wide open. This is because you can do small favors for targets with the knowledge that you can ask for a very much larger favor in return[82]. You can cleverly leverage the principle of reciprocity to your own advantage.

- *Example: Always be Mr. Helpful.* Discover your target's deepest interests and strongest motivations. Then vigilantly scout out opportunities to do them favors based on your sophisticated knowledge of their personality.

- *Example: Act like a gentleman.* Remember small courtesies, keep your word, honor your promises, and if you do something wrong then sincerely apologize for it. When you act decently toward others, then they, by and large, respond in more-than-equal measure. "Do unto others as you would have them do unto you," as Luke says in the Bible.

- *Example: Use the door-in-the-face tactic.* This is a clever strategy for gaining concessions. After your target is first given the opportunity to turn down a large request (the door initially slamming in your face), you then nimbly counteroffer with a smaller appeal. The target is much more likely to accept the smaller request after the previous larger demand was made. For example:

---

[82] Gouldner, Alvin W. "The norm of reciprocity: A preliminary statement." *American sociological review* (1960): 161-178.

- *Large request*: Can you invest $300,000 in our business?

- *Smaller request*: No, well how about $30,000? (which is the sum you really wanted in the first place)

- The power of the door-in-the-face technique is partly due to the principle of reciprocity. The target feels that they "owe you" due to the fact that they rejected the first and larger offer, so they are compelled to make a concession and accept the reduced request.

Also, compared to the original appeal, the second request appears eminently reasonable because it is relatively smaller. This is known as the contrast principle. Therefore, you are more likely to accept the second bid when it cheekily follows a large proposition as opposed to when it is just made on its own[83].

---

[83] Cialdini, Robert B., Joyce E. Vincent, Stephen K. Lewis, Jose Catalan, Diane Wheeler, and Betty Lee Darby. "Reciprocal concessions procedure for inducing compliance: The door-in-the-face technique." *Journal of personality and Social Psychology* 31, no. 2 (1975): 206.

E PERSUASION WEAPON NUMBER FIVE: ACCESSING THE SUBCONSCIOUS MIND

In the freewheeling 1980s, ambitious property brokers carved out a lucrative niche cold-calling wealthy potential clients to sell them time-share apartments. Initially the brokers mistakenly believed that the best way to peddle their (often dubious) wares was to inform customers about the wonderful features of their products, such as the generous size of the properties, the stunningly favorable locations, the amazingly competitive prices, and so on.

However, through painstaking trial and error, they eventually realized that their efforts were often falling on deaf ears. This approach just wasn't bringing home the bacon. They eventually discovered that the key to consistently landing the big sales was to "sell the sizzle, not the steak." In other words, they needed to create a captivating and enticing image in the mind of the customer about how buying the time-share would transform their lifestyle for the better. One broker told me *"Once I started doing this my profits absolutely soared".*

The twenty-first century is the information age. We are constantly bombarded with a humongous quantity of sensory data. There is so much that it is literally impossible to make sense of it all. In order to cope, the beleaguered brain filters out much of this information. The mind naturally focuses on, and is drawn to, stuff that stands out as being engaging, memorable, and attention grabbing, or in other words "salient." It simply discards everything else. It follows that to successfully control your target's mind, you must turbocharge the salience of your persuasion[84]. Next I will divulge the secrets of how this is done.

PAINT A BEAUTIFUL VERBAL PICTURE

A picture paints a thousand words, but words can also craft a striking mental picture. Metaphors, similes, and personifications allow you to describe novel or complicated concepts and objects in terms of familiar mental images. This improves the effectiveness of your persuasion because it is easier for the target to understand and accept[85].

So what exactly are metaphors, similes, and personifications? My apologies to those readers who already know. Metaphors

---

[84] Petty, Richard E., and John T. Cacioppo. "The effects of involvement on responses to argument quantity and quality: Central and peripheral routes to persuasion." *Journal of personality and social psychology* 46, no. 1 (1984): 69.

[85] Charteris-Black, Jonathan. *Politicians and rhetoric: The persuasive power of metaphor.* (2005)

state that one concept or thing *is* another. For example, "Love *is* a journey," or "Love *is* sugar sweet." Similes differ in that they use words such as "like" or "as." For example, "Love is *like* a journey" or "*as* sweet *as* sugar." Finally personification gives *human characteristics* to concepts and ideas. For example, "Love took the first tentative steps on its long journey." This personification describes the concept of love as if it were an actual human who walks and behaves "tentatively". More examples of these three closely related literary techniques are given below.

METAPHOR EXAMPLES

- Each business success buys an admission ticket to a more difficult problem.

- He's got a wonderful head for money. There's a long slit on the top.

- Business is a combination of war and sport.

SIMILE EXAMPLES

- Trading without advertising *is like* winking at a girl in the dark—you know you are doing it, but nobody else does.

- Working in that office *was like* going daily to the dentist for root canal surgery on the same tooth.

- Anyone who plays the stock market and is not an insider *is like* someone who buys cows in the moonlight.

PERSONIFICATION EXAMPLES

- Opportunity began to *knock on my door*.

- The stock market *rallied* today.

- Fortune *favors* the brave.

- Lady Luck is *smiling* on you.

CREATE GRIPPING IMAGES IN THE MIND'S EYE

Another frankly ingenious method of adding sparkle to your persuasive message is to pepper it with practical "real-life" illustrations. Targets are able to clearly visualize these pictures in their mind's eye and therefore find them easy to relate to[86].

There are three ways of incorporating illustrations into your persuasive toolbox. First of all, you can tell a spellbinding *story* about what happened to you or to another person in the past. Second, you can request the target to vividly imagine a certain situation happening, either to them, you, or another person. This is known as *guided visualization*. In addition you can expertly use *visual props* to hammer home your point.

---

[86] Brosius, Hans-Bernd, and Anke Bathelt. "The utility of exemplars in persuasive communications." *Communication Research* 21, no. 1 (1994): 48-78.

STORIES

The human brain is hardwired for attraction to storytelling. This goes back to prehistoric caveman times, when primitive man huddled around the blazing campfire, listening to intrepid hunters tell lurid tales about their brave exploits of slaying ferocious woolly mammoths.

Stories pack a powerful punch in a variety of persuasive contexts—in sales testimonials, in public speaking; even the parables in the Bible are a form of story which aim to persuade you of their underlying religious truths. You really would be a crazy fool not to include the potent technique of storytelling in your arsenal of persuasion weapons[87].

Let me give you a business-related example of how to use storytelling to persuade; imagine that you want to sell your target a round-the-world luxury cruise. This trip would be an utterly unforgettable experience, but it would require him to spend most of his carefully amassed life savings.

To clinch the sale, you would need to persuade him to buy into the philosophy that he should "enjoy life" and "live for today." You

---

[87] McKee, Robert, and Bronwyn Fryer. "Storytelling that moves people." *Harvard Business Review* 81, no. 6 (2003): 51-55.

could use a story, like this one below; to help you hit pay dirt: "I knew someone just like you. He was a really wonderful friend of mine, who I met at college, named Bob. He didn't drink, smoke, or eat meat. His motto in life was 'Just play it safe.' He was so damn sensible that he wouldn't even drive one mile per hour over the speed limit or go out on his own after dark. Caution was most certainly his watchword".

"Confident in his "total risk avoidance" approach to life, he fully expected to live until he was at least one hundred years old. Sadly tragedy stuck. Would you believe that he dropped stone-cold dead from a heart attack at just forty? It goes to show that you should enjoy life while you still can!"

Let's consider another example. Suppose that you are attempting to sell real estate to a potential buy-to-lease investor. This target is initially stubbornly reluctant to accept your carefully honed pitch. He sensibly suspects that returns from alternative investments, such as stocks, could outperform the rental income which your property could potentially earn him. You could have him considering the flip side through a story like this to clinch the deal:

"You really don't want to make the same stupid mistake as my uncle Joe. His firm gave him an $85,000 early retirement package when he lost his job as an accountant. He quarreled at length with his wife over how he should invest the money. He wanted to invest it in property, and his wife preferred to put it in

213

stocks. As is often the case, his wife won the argument hands-down.

"Unfortunately Joe's stockbroker grossly mismanaged his money and within three years, he got wiped out—his portfolio value dropped to only $27,000. But Joe's shrewder colleague, who also lost his job at the same time and received a similar early retirement package, wisely invested his funds in bricks and mortar. Over the same period, he made a profit of $25,000, giving him a total of $110,000."

The moral of that story is, as far as investments are concerned, there really is nothing "as safe as houses."

The more details you can weave into your story, the more plausible and beguiling your alternate approach will appear to be to your target, and the more likely you are to sway them.

GUIDED VISUALIZATION

Another way to mix some zing into your communication is to employ the stunningly effective guided visualization technique[88].

---

[88] MacInnis, Deborah J., and Linda L. Price. "The role of imagery in information processing: Review and extensions." *Journal of consumer research* (1987): 473-491.

Here you invite the target to vividly *imagine* the situation which you are trying to explain or the incentive which you are offering them. To fully exploit the power of this method, you need to teasingly titillate, to the max, all of the senses: seeing, hearing, smelling, feeling, and tasting.

For instance, to entice a key player in your industry to join you for a vital networking dinner, you could say something like:

"Imagine seeing the seductive red wine sparkling in the glass, the aroma of delicious food wafting through the air, the delicious taste of a rich chocolate desert, classical music setting a delectably sophisticated ambiance, and the luxurious sensation of the soft leather seats on your skin."

Or to give another example, to coax them into cruising on your luxury yacht, you might tempt them with the following verbal imagery:

"Picture the deep azure-blue sea stretching out for miles around you as you cut effortlessly across the ocean, the sound of the waves crashing gently against the side of the boat, the intoxicating scent and tang of sea salt drifting in the air, and the sensual feel of the polished sheesham wood on the ship's wheel."

USING VISUAL PROPS

You can cleverly employ props and visual aids such as photographs, video, audio, and so on, to beef up your communication[89]. For instance, a canny dentist could highlight his unsurpassed professional expertise by prominently displaying pictures of two sets of teeth in the window of his dental practice. He could label one set of choppers, which are shockingly disgusting and rotten, as "pretreatment" and the other set of teeth, which look immaculately pristine and healthy, as "post-treatment." This would showcase his skills much more influentially as opposed to just verbally describing the services he provides.

STIR A SMIDGEN OF SPICE INTO YOUR PERSUASION DISH

Vibrant and colorful adjectives (describing words) are like a shot of dope to the target's senses, and invoke an automatic and potent emotional response, helping you to influence them.

---

[89] Joffe, Hélène. "The power of visual material: Persuasion, emotion and identification." *Diogenes* 55, no. 1 (2008): 84-93.

So don't blandly say to your client, "If you award me this contract, I guarantee that I will provide a good service." Instead guarantee a "VIP service" or a "gold standard" service or a "platinum" service. You are essentially saying the same thing, but it sounds much better when using juicier adjectives. Utilising vivid adjectives in this way will make your persuasive skills sharper than a cutthroat razor. Some examples of vivid adjectives are given below:

- Adorable
- Beautiful
- Smart
- Superb
- Glorious
- Outstanding
- Chic
- Stylish
- Graceful

- Elegant
- Exotic
- Luxurious
- Extravagant
- Well-appointed
- Lavish
- Plush
- Sparkling
- Timeles

STAND ON THE MIGHTY SHOULDERS OF PERSUASION GIANTS

You can use quotations, misquotations, and allusions to audaciously borrow from unquestionable sources of authority, thereby bolstering your own perceived credibility[90]. First of all let's consider *quotations*. Your communication message sounds more plausible if a famous and respected person has made a similar point as you before but expressed it considerably more eloquently and profoundly. Therefore, use quotations by legendary individuals to "borrow legitimacy and prestige" for your persuasion efforts.

For example, to persuade a target to join you in a business venture, you could use the following quotations:

> There are risks and costs to a program of action, but they are far less than the long-range risks and costs of comfortable inaction.
>
> —John F. Kennedy
>
> And the day came when the risk to remain tight in a bud was more painful than the risk it took to blossom.
>
> —Anaïs Nin

---

[90] Gibson, Rhonda, and Dolf Zillmann. "The impact of quotation in news reports on issue perception." *Journalism & Mass Communication Quarterly* 70, no. 4 (1993): 793-800.

Great deeds are usually wrought at great risks.

—Herodotus

Alternatively, to emphasize to a target the importance of "making the most of their life," you could use the following quotes:

Life is like a coin. You can spend it any way you wish, but you only spend it once.

—Lillian Dickson

Life is the game that must be played.

—Edwin Arlington Robinson

You will never be happy if you continue to search for what happiness consists of. You will never live if you are looking for the meaning of life.

—Albert Camus

Misquotations are also persuasion dynamite. For example, consider this well-known quote about the benefit of taking immediate action:

Never leave that till tomorrow which you can do today.

—Benjamin Franklin

You can skillfully modify this to humorously persuade the target of the advantage of *not* being hasty (notice the <u>underlined text</u>):

> Never leave that till tomorrow which you can do <u>next month</u>.

Or consider the following well-known quote about the gains enjoyed by those who make an early start to the day:

> Early to bed and early to rise, makes a man healthy, wealthy, and wise.
>
> —Benjamin Franklin

You can tweak this to lightheartedly convey to the target that it is essential to relax rather than to work too hard (notice the <u>underlined text</u>):

> Early to bed and early to rise, makes a man healthy, wealthy, and <u>boring</u>.

An *allusion* is a close linguistic relative of a quotation, except it is a reference to an iconic work of art, literary work, event, or place rather than simply something that a famous person has sagely uttered. The Bible and other religious texts are a veritable gold mine of allusions. For example, you could use the following biblical allusions to persuade a target to take a risk:

Don't worry about tomorrow because tomorrow will look after itself.

Don't hide your light under a bushel.

USE SNAZZY, SNAPPY SLOGANS

Astute advertisers know that a brilliant method of enhancing the power of your persuasion is to spring out a snappy slogan[91]. For example, Nike's renowned "Just Do It" and Adidas's "Impossible Is Nothing" are both legendary. Other famous examples include Apple's "Think Different" or the British SAS's "Who Dares Wins."

There are six amazing techniques for developing memorable and snappy slogans, and, therefore, increasing the likelihood of achieving your persuasive aims.

---

[91] Dolan, P., M. Hallsworth, D. Halpern, D. King, and D. Vlaev. "MINDSPACE: Influencing behaviour through public policy. 2010." *Cabinet Office and Institute for Government, London, UK.*

ALLITERATION

This is where you repeat the sound of the first consonants in a series of phrases or words. For example: Credit Crunch, Buy British, Coffee Corner, or Sushi Station. When you adroitly put words together like this, they latch onto a target's subconscious like a feisty little limpet.

THE RULE OF THREE

Laying concepts into groups of three is an especially effective persuasion gambit. Slippery politicians are infamous for using and abusing this method. Barack Obama flogged this technique to death in his election campaign speeches. Well-known examples of the rule of three include:

- I came. I saw. I conquered.

- Father, Son, and Holy Spirit

- The good, the bad, and the ugly

- Turn on, tune in, and drop out

- Sex, drugs, and rock and roll

SEQUENCES

Using sequences of concepts rocket-powers your persuasive abilities (notice the <u>underlined text</u>):

> I live alone with my cat. At <u>twenty-seven</u> that's nothing. At <u>thirty-seven</u> no big deal. At <u>forty-seven</u> really difficult.
>
> —Tracy Emin
>
> My week went from bad to worse. On <u>Monday</u> I was happy. On <u>Tuesday</u> I felt a bit deflated. On <u>Wednesday</u> I felt glum. On <u>Thursday</u> I felt rather blue. On <u>Friday</u> I felt sad. On <u>Saturday</u> I was depressed, and on <u>Sunday</u> I was suicidal.
>
> —Anonymous

REPETITION

This is where you repeat a phrase or word several times over to forcefully pound your message home (notice the <u>underlined text</u>):

> We shall <u>fight</u> on the beaches. We shall <u>fight</u> on the landing grounds. We shall <u>fight</u> in the fields and in the

streets. We shall <u>fight</u> in the hills. We shall never surrender.

—Winston Churchill

What <u>lies</u> behind us and what <u>lies </u>before us are tiny compared to what <u>lies</u> within us.

—Ralph Waldo Emerson

And the <u>world</u> said, "Disarm, disclose, or face serious consequences"—and, therefore, we worked with the <u>world</u>. We worked to make sure that Saddam Hussein heard the message of the <u>world</u>.

—George W. Bush

Rock-and-roll journalism is <u>people</u> who can't write, interviewing <u>people</u> who can't talk, for <u>people</u> who can't read.

—Frank Zappa

CONTRASTS

This is the opposite of using similes in that it shows how two things are *different* rather than highlighting how two things are *the same*. For example:

- In theory/in practice

- According to the popular view/in reality

- In the past/in the present

- In the present/in the future

- In Europe /in America

RHETORICAL QUESTIONS

This is where you pose a question deliberately to add emphasis to your persuasive message rather than expecting a reply. The aim is to get the target thinking about what the answer to the question might be. Examples include:

- How much longer are you going to suffer injustice? (Don't continue to suffer injustice.)

- Do you want to stay a loser all your life? (Don't be a loser all your life.)

- What did the Romans do for us? (The Romans didn't do anything for us.)

GAMIFY YOUR COMMUNICATION

A scorching-hot topic in marketing at the moment is the concept of "gamification"[92] This is all about harnessing the addictive properties of computer games to influence your target audience. As gaming becomes increasingly realistic, many people (especially in Japan apparently) are absolutely hooked on technologically created fantasy personas that live in virtual worlds. They have come to be fully absorbed in these cyberuniverses as they become masters of their own artificial domain, progressing through levels, vanquishing enemies, amassing wealth and rewards, and earning special powers.

There are two main methods of employing the habit-forming power of gamification in your communication. First of all, set challenges and goals to attain for the target, providing scores

---

[92] Llagostera, Enric. "On gamification and persuasion." *SB Games, Brasilia, Brazil, November 2-4 2012* (2012): 12-21.

and rewards based on their performance. Let's say that you are selling the target a car. Gamification would involve saying things like: "I bet you can't guess how much of a discount I am offering on this car. Is it 10, 20, or 30 percent? If you get the answer right, I will throw in a free pair of driving gloves!" or "If you spend $750 USD in my shop this month, you become a VIP customer. If you spend $7,500 USD you are designated a Gold VIP client, and if you spend $15,000 USD, you join the exclusive elite of Platinum VIP patrons."

The second method is to ask your targets to perform cute little role-plays. For instance, you could say something like this to them: "Let's pretend that you are my boss and you are mad about the massive discount that I am giving to the customer on this car. I am practically cutting my own throat. What sort of profane names would you be calling me?" or "Let's imagine you are laying happily on the beach, sipping a delicious cocktail, surrounded by a bevy of fine-looking women, having a whale of a time spending the enormous profits of this business venture. How great would you be feeling?"

IF THEY'RE LAUGHING, YOU'RE LAUGHING

George Bernard Shaw once said, "If you're going to tell people the truth, you'd better make them laugh. Otherwise, they'll kill you." When used effectively, humor is like a warming shot of persuasion whiskey. It dissolves social barriers, melts away anxiety, generates a warm glow, and helps forge the bonds of long-lasting friendships[93]. So dust off your favorite comedy DVDs and get practicing! A point to note is that, when using humor to persuade, a clever trick is to use the "sandwich approach." Make your point, use humor to illustrate it, and then make your point once again.

---

[93] Weinberger, Marc G., and Charles S. Gulas. "The impact of humor in advertising: A review." *Journal of Advertising* 21, no. 4 (1992): 35-59.

F PERSUASION WEAPON NUMBER SIX: PROVING POPULARITY

Sheep are somewhat curious creatures. Observe them while they are peacefully grazing, and you will notice that they invariably group together in a little bunch. They are strongly disposed to follow the sheep in front of them. If the herd starts moving in a certain direction, then all the sheep will dutifully follow, even when it means mindlessly following the flock to a grisly death (e.g., jumping straight off a cliff!).

This instinct is genetically hardwired into sheep because they are vulnerable "prey animals." They band together to escape dangerous predators, such as coyotes, dogs, and mountain lions and maximize their survival chances. Cold-blooded predators will always attack the outliers in the flock first. Therefore the risk-averse sheep stay in the safest place, which is right in the center of the herd[94].

---

[94] King, Andrew J., Alan M. Wilson, Simon D. Wilshin, John Lowe, Hamed Haddadi, Stephen Hailes, and A. Jennifer Morton. "Selfish-herd behaviour of sheep under threat." *Current Biology* 22, no. 14 (2012): R561-R562.

Actually humans aren't that much different from sheep in this respect. In many situations, they also thoughtlessly look to others to decide what to do and slavishly copy their behavior. They sense that this is safer than being an "outlier"—thinking and acting independently, and relying on their own good judgment. This psychological phenomenon is known as "herd behavior". It is most common in uncertain or unfamiliar social situations, where individuals lack the necessary knowledge about how to behave appropriately[95].

It is easy to observe herd behavior in the Darwinian jungle of work and business. For instance, you must have seen a situation where there is two very similar restaurants, selling the same type of food and located near each other, but one is packed to the rafters, and the other doesn't have a soul in it? This is usually because of the ubiquitous phenomenon of herd behavior.

Put yourself in the hungry customer's shoes. Imagine that you fancy a bite to eat. You set out into town to purchase yourself a tasty meal. You stroll past two similar restaurants, lazily pondering which one to go to. Since you have never patronized either establishment before, you don't know in advance which one serves the better quality fare. What you are likely to do in this case is simply peer in the restaurant windows, see which

---

[95] Cialdini, Robert B. *Influence.* (1987)

one is the busiest, and, like a good sheep, follow the rest of the human herd.

Clever restaurant owners know that this is how people commonly make decisions and often strategically place their customers near their window, in full sight of hungry potential patrons.

It's not only in the cut-and-thrust world of commerce that herd behavior casts its powerful spell. What do you think is the best method of attracting the most stunning guy or girl in the nightclub? It's to hang out with other fine lookers, of course! When you are seen surrounded by the beautiful people, then you are perceived as being "a somebody" and, therefore, of high status and highly desirable.

You can practice a variety of fiendish tricks to leverage herd behavior to persuade others:

- *Example: Use testimonials.* For instance, if you run your own business, then prominently display positive feedback from satisfied consumers on your website in the form of text or videos. Ask loyal friends and clients to produce articles or videos, all bursting full of gushing praise about your business, and have them post these online themselves. Similarly request customers to provide glowing reviews for your product (e.g. on the popular online sales platform Amazon).

- *Example: Use recommendations.* Ask your clients if they

will recommend your services to their good friends. Their buddies are much more likely to buy something from you if one of their close chums has endorsed it than if you just approach them cold.

- *Example: Display user statistics.* If you rack up tons of product sales or are inundated with a constant deluge of hits on your business website, then why not let your customers know about it? It would be terribly rude not to. For example, McDonald's uses the phrase "Billions and billions served" in their marketing to help them shift more Big Macs.

- *Example: Use social marketing buzz.* This is a similar concept to using recommendations. Ask your überloyal customers to promote your product for you, via word of mouth, though social media platforms, such as Facebook and Twitter

- *Example: Cultivate the impression that anyone who is anyone knows you.* For example, weave elaborate stories about the exciting and high-profile events you grace with your presence, and the famous and glamorous circles you move in.

- *Example: Create a huge virtual social or business circle.* Invite the world and his wife to become your friend or link to you on social networking sites. This will make you appear to be the most well-networked player in your industry and will keep the cash registers singing merrily away.

- *Example: Use social proof to steer customers to your most expensive products.* Use phrases like "This is our most popular product" or "This is the product which the majority of our customers like best" to inspire extra sales.

G PERSUASION WEAPON NUMBER SEVEN: OBLIGATING TO OBTAIN COMMITMENT

"A gentleman's word is his bond" is an old-fashioned maxim which essentially means that a promise given by a man of honor is a promise invariably kept. Paying a bond is completely unnecessary for someone with these old-school values. He would never, even for a moment, contemplate breaking his word and sullying his good name.

In Europe, this tradition of honorably keeping one's word goes back to pre-Christian pagan times, when it was widely believed that oath-breakers would pay the grim price of damnation to eternal hellfire. There are similar traditions in ancient cultures all over the globe.

Even today, society generally cherishes those individuals who are consistent in their words and actions. Those who "do what they say and say what they do" are seen as solid, dependable, and morally virtuous. On the other hand, we generally despise inconsistent people, especially those who don't keep their word. We view them as weak, flaky, and morally suspect, and eventually we shun them as social lepers.

Because of this, most people strive to behave consistently, even if this involves significant personal costs[96].

Scientists demonstrated the magnetic power of the desire for consistency in a renowned experiment called the Beach Towel Study.[97] This research involved leaving a beach towel next to an arbitrary stranger and strolling off along the beach. One randomly selected group was asked for a commitment: "Could you please watch my things?" Another similar group was not asked for any commitment. The scientists then faked an attempted theft of the beach towel; the part of the would-be thief was played by an actor.

Nine out of ten people who made the commitment gallantly tried to halt the villain by physically restraining him or chasing him bravely down the beach. However, only one in five of the group who was not asked for a commitment tried to stop the crook from pilfering the towel.

This experiment shows that once someone makes a commitment (e.g., pledges to guard the towel), they will often take significant

---

[96] Ibid

[97] Moriarty, T., "Crime, Commitment, and the Responsive Bystander: Two Field Experiments," *Journal of Personality and Social Psychology* 31 (1975): 370–376.

personal risks (e.g., tackling a potentially dangerous felon) to honor their earlier promise.

The potent human desire for consistency is a convenient lever which you can use to ensure psychological compliance. When people don't live up to their commitments, they experience a highly unpleasant sensation known as cognitive dissonance. Individuals tend to agree to things which aren't at all in their best interests to avoid this very disagreeable feeling.

This is how it works. You get your target to make a small initial commitment. You then make larger requests that are in line with that first promise. The target is much more likely to agree to these bigger requests if they have made the earlier pledge (to avoid cognitive dissonance) than if they were just asked for the big fat request straight-out[98].

For example, charity fund-raisers work like horses at persuading people to sign petitions (e.g., protecting rare animals, helping vulnerable children, and so on). Many people mistakenly think that fund-raisers do this because amassing stacks of signatures on a petition will win the hearts and minds of political kingpins, persuading them to back the charity. Please don't be deceived! The real reason that the fund-raisers want Joe Public's signature

---

[98] Bryan, Gharad, Dean Karlan, and Scott Nelson. "Commitment devices." *Annu. Rev. Econ.* 2, no. 1 (2010): 671-698.

on that form is that it represents a small initial psychological commitment to support their cause.

Once the gullible citizen has taken this first step, it is much easier to ask for a much more significant request (i.e., a substantial financial contribution) later down the line. This is because, once they have signed the petition, *they start to think of themselves* as someone who cares about helping vulnerable children, protecting animals, and so on. This makes them much more likely to put their hand in their pocket and donate, to avoid the dreaded cognitive dissonance that arises from acting inconsistently with this newly created self-image. So the *real* reason that crafty charity fund-raisers are so desperate to get signatures on those ever-present appeals is to deliberately exploit the human desire for consistency.

Here are three killer techniques which you can use to harness the amazing power of psychological consistency:

- *Example: Use the foot-in-the-door technique.* This procedure is explained in the previous example about the charity fund-raisers[99].

---

[99] Freedman, Jonathan L., and Scott C. Fraser. "Compliance without pressure: the foot-in-the-door technique." *Journal of personality and social psychology* 4, no. 2 (1966): 195.

- *Example: Use the bait-and-switch technique*[100]. Another persuasion tactic relating to the consistency principle is the bait-and-switch technique. First of all, you make the target an attractive offer (tantalizingly dangle the bait). Make it enticing enough that they bite but not so unbelievably good that the offer lacks credibility. Once the target accepts the proposal, you immediately get them to commit, either verbally or in writing, to the purchase. This ensures buy-in.

- Then switch to an arrangement which favors you at their expense. As long as the offer which the target gets after the switch is not ridiculously inferior, they might whine a bit, but will probably grudgingly accept it. Bait-and-switch works because once the target commits to the purchase they behave consistently to avoid cognitive dissonance from their initial commitment, even if they get a raw deal.

- Unscrupulous real estate agents make regular use of bait-and-switch. When they show gullible prospective buyers around a property, they initially quote a low price as "bait." Once the interested customer commits to buy, the agent then sneakily asks for a higher price (switching

---

[100] Lazear, Edward P. "Bait and switch." *Journal of Political Economy* (1995): 813-830

the deal). Because buyers act consistently with their earlier belief of wanting to buy the property, they often cough up the extra amount.

- *Example: Persuade the target to make commitments publicly and in writing*[101]. Commitments are more effective if made in front of others and/or in writing. For instance, if you are attempting to sell the target a product, start off by asking them to describe what they like about it, putting to one side for the time being the things that they don't like. Once they have made that public commitment to admiring the product, at least in some respects, you significantly up their chances of buying.

---

[101] Hoy, Wayne K., and Page A. Smith. "Influence: a key to successful leadership." *International journal of educational management* 21, no. 2 (2007): 158-167.

H PERSUASION WEAPON NUMBER EIGHT: NUDGING USING INCENTIVES

Do you know what radio station most people listen to? It's WII FM Radio. This stands for What's In It For Me? We all look after *numero uno*, so to persuade your target effectively, you must give them a sufficiently compelling *incentive* to do your bidding.

WIELD THE STICK AND DANGLE THE CARROT

Imagine a rider on a stubborn old donkey. To control the animal, he must either tantalizingly dangle a scrumptious carrot in front of its nose or ferociously beat it with a stick. The carrot is a *positive* incentive; it plays on the donkey's gluttonous lust for the pleasure of eating. On the other hand, the stick is a *negative* incentive; it exploits the donkey's terror of a painful strike from the stick.

For all their apparent sophistication and complexity, humans habitually behave in a remarkably similar way to the donkey. They are often driven by a cowardly fear of pain (*negative* incentives) and an ignoble greed for pleasure (*positive* incentives)[102].

As Jeremy Bentham, a famous economist puts it, "Nature has placed mankind under the governance of two sovereign masters, pain and pleasure. It is for them alone to point out what we ought to do, as well as to determine what we shall do."[103]

I will reveal the secret of how to use incentives to devastating effect, starting with the very basics. You might want to persuade a target to:

- Buy from you at a fantastic price

- Sell to you at a rock-bottom price

- Work for your company

---

[102] Laffont, Jean-Jacques, and David Martimort. *The theory of incentives: the principal-agent model* (2009)

[103] Bentham, Jeremy. *An introduction to the principles of morals and legislation* (2007).

- Provide a glowing endorsement for your company

- Date you

- Introduce you to the big players in your industry

An incentive can involve giving or taking something of monetary value from the target (*external incentive*) or just invoking certain emotional feelings (an *internal incentive*) to get them to follow your wishes.

CROSSING THEIR PALMS WITH SILVER

Bribing the target with money or something of monetary value is known as a "positive external incentive." This can include gifting them *products*, such as a box of luxury chocolates, fine cigars, or an antique painting. It can also involve treating them to an exciting *experience*, such as an all-expenses-paid day at the races, an appointment with an exclusive hair stylist, ringside seats at a world title fight, or tickets to a hip music gig. Examples of external incentives include:

- Money

- Shopping vouchers

- Food

- Sex

- A pleasurable experience, such as watching a movie or listening to music

- A massage

A negative external incentive would involve a cost to the target of some kind. For instance:

- A fine

- A charge

- An increased price

- Taking something away that they own or that you said you were going to give them

DELICATELY STROKE THEIR EGO

Shameless bribery will surely get you a long way in life. There is much truth in William Andrews Clark's witty quip when he was caught red-handed in a bribery scandal during a campaign for a US Senate seat: "I never bought a man who wasn't for sale."

But individuals don't purely base their decisions on a cold, hardheaded, logical analysis of the material payoff of a particular course of action. Emotions and moods also hold great sway. The human decision-making process is more akin to Homer Simpson than *Star Trek*'s Mr. Spock. As Jared Diamond once said, "Perhaps our greatest distinction as a species is our capacity, unique among animals, to make counterevolutionary choices."[104] Put differently, we often act against our own best interests, because our emotional and passionate nature overrides our faculties of reason and common sense.

Internal incentives relate to emotional feelings—which flower from the seeds of the targets' egos— their concept of themselves. Internal incentives either provide a boost (a positive incentive) or a blow (a negative incentive) to their ego[105].

---

[104] Diamond.Jared. *Why Is Sex Fun?* (1998)

[105] Johnson, B.T. and A.H. Eagly. "Effects of involvement on persuasion: A meta-analysis." *Psychological Bulletin* 106, no. 2 (1989): 290.

EXAMPLES OF POSITIVE INTERNAL INCENTIVES

This type of incentive works by making the targets feel like a million dollars (on the condition that they do what you want of course). For example, it makes them feel:

- Sexually attractive

- Socially important and popular

- Moral, noble, and honorable

- Wealthy

- Intelligent

- Brave

- A tough guy

- Cool or exciting

- Talented

A positive incentive would involve saying something like "Only the coolest and hippest people buy from me" to sell more products. Or "I can see that you are a person of great integrity,

246

so I know you will offer me a fair deal," to get a rock-bottom price. Or, to give another example, you can use "I know you will offer me this deal because one talented person recognizes another one" to help land a dream contract.

EXAMPLES OF NEGATIVE INTERNAL INCENTIVES

This type of incentive makes the target feel like the dirt on someone's shoe. Negative internal incentives exert a surprisingly dominant effect on decision making. These incentives involve saying or implying that, if you don't follow my wishes, you must be:

- Repulsive to the opposite sex

- Unpopular or unimportant

- Poor and low status

- Stupid

- Cowardly

- Weak

- Boring and unfashionable

- Mediocre

- A bad person

This could involve saying something like "Will you date me, or are you too boring to be with a bad guy/girl?" or "Only a coward would miss out on this extraordinary business opportunity," or "I am confident that you will loan me this money, because I know you aren't a bad friend."

AIMING STRAIGHT FOR THE HEART OF THE TARGET'S CORE IDENTITY

Now let me share a piece of occult knowledge that the great marketing gurus in history have all intimately known. The first part of this secret is that every last soul in the big wide world, no matter who they are and where they come from, *wants to feel like a somebody.* As American philosopher John Dewey puts it, "The deepest urge in human nature is the desire to be important."[106] The second part is that, to satisfy their fragile egos, people create self-aggrandizing identities as vehicles for achieving this sense of importance.

---

[106] Dale Carnegie, *How to Win Friends and Influence People* (1936).

For instance, someone with an aptitude for making and performing music or for writing might construct himself a core identity as "a creative." A gentleman who thrives in the corporate environment might fashion a core identity as a "hardheaded business executive." A lady who plays a fine game of tennis might build up a core identity as a "sportswoman."

Core identities are nourishing food and drink to the individuals' egos, as they project a self-promoting image to the rest of society about why they are worthy of esteem.

For example, budding writers will carefully nurture a core identity as "a creative" because it is on that basis which society is most likely to afford them the respect they crave. They might be a bone-idle waster without two pennies to rub together, and they might have always gotten picked last for the school football teams. Nevertheless they are *creative*, and, therefore, they are *a somebody* in their own world.

Similarly a talented tennis player might be an entry-level secretary when at work, but when she grabs her racket and heads onto the court, she is a feared and respected opponent. Therefore, she will cling like a limpet to her core identity as a sportswoman to defend her ego.

To make your internal incentives more potent, you must fire them like a deadly arrow straight at the heart of your target's core identity.

Your first step is to understand how your targets *see themselves*, which is how they want other people to see them too. This is as easy as falling off a log because every time people open their mouths, they are actually frantically trying to project their self-image to others.

For example, a guy with a core identity as a high-flying city trader will constantly boast about money and making deals. A person who self-identifies as a "party animal" will routinely regale others with decadent tales of his hedonistic exploits. A self-proclaimed "bad guy" will incessantly brag about his daring capers and hair-raising brushes with the law and so on.

You can also make an impressionistic judgment on targets' core identities from how they dress and the company they keep. For instance, a "party animal" might wear showy and flamboyant clothes and hang out with wildly extroverted and crazy people. On the other hand, an "artist" may shun any trappings of materialistic society (e.g., designer labels) and sit in chic cafés wearing Buddy Holly glasses, loafers with no socks, and a paisley shirt (or whatever is currently in vogue for this fickle social demographic). Therefore, finding out a target's core identity is a piece of cake with a bit of mildly intelligent detective work.

The next step is to cleverly rustle up an incentive (either positive or negative) which speaks loudly and clearly to that core identity.

For instance, a self-styled "sportswoman" would be almost

powerless to resist either a positive incentive which paints a picture of her as a great athlete (e.g., winning an award or some other type of affirmative recognition) or a negative incentive which belittles her sporting prowess (e.g., criticism of a recent sports performance). These sorts of incentives are as explosive as C-4 because they go to the very core of the target's soul.

However, if you instead use an incentive which related to that very same person's ability as an "artist," then it would fall as flat as a pancake. Since she sees herself as a "sportswoman" rather than an "artist," this inducement would do nothing to persuade her to follow your whims. Therefore, it is very important that you select an incentive which resonates with your target.

TO BE A GOOD FISHERMAN, YOU MUST CHOOSE YOUR BAIT CAREFULLY

This point about calibrating your approach to suit your target has wider applications. Any good angler will tell you that the most effective way to catch fish is to skillfully vary your choice of bait, depending on the circumstances. Sometimes they will use shiny metal bait, sometimes wriggling earthworms, sometimes slithering maggots, sometimes little chunks of stale bread, and so on.

If one type of bait isn't successfully getting the obstinate fishes to bite, then the expert fisherman will nonchalantly shrug his shoulders and load up his rod with something else.

The same principle applies when baiting your target with incentives. The optimal choice of incentives to use (i.e., positive versus negative, internal versus external, and so on) depends mostly on the situation. You must first consider carefully which type of incentive to use, based on a sophisticated understanding of the target, and flexibly change tack if your initial approach isn't getting bites. You must bait the hook to suit the fish.

Generally speaking, internal incentives are more effective at influencing the more emotional and altruistic minded, while external incentives are more tempting to those of a relatively covetous and materialistic nature.

Some targets are more juiced up by cash, others by fast cars, others by jewelry, others by exciting experiences, and so on. Therefore, it is important to understand "what makes the target tick" to focus your incentives with laserlike precision.

- *Example:* Explicitly consider how to harness the magic of incentives to successfully persuade your targets. Understand *what's in it for them?* Consider what money, goods, and services you can grease their palms with (external incentives) and how you can adroitly massage their ego (internal incentives).

ONLY STRIKE WHILE THE IRON IS HOT

Please note that incentives do not operate in an emotional vacuum. The targets' current emotional state is a powerful driver of their decision-making process. If you catch targets when they have gotten up on the wrong side of bed, then *you* are going to fall flat on your face[107].

- *Example:* Deftly gauge your targets' emotional state before you attempt to influence them. Focus your persuasion efforts on those times when they are feeling good. Back off when they are in a bad mood and wait for a more opportune moment.

---

[107] Jorgensen, Peter F. "Affect, persuasion, and communication processes." (1998).

FEAR IS STRONGER THAN GREED

It's important to know how to present external incentives. As any good Gordon Gekko–esque trader knows, humans are primarily driven by the base and ignoble emotions of fear and greed[108]. Interestingly, evidence shows that when these two emotions go head-to-head, fear comes out on top every time. The *fear* of losing something already in their sweaty clutches (i.e., a *negative* incentive) sways your targets' thought processes more than the *greed* of getting their hands on something new (i.e., a *positive* incentive).

To illustrate, academic studies show that individuals are, on average, more upset about losing $10 (negative incentive) than they are pleased to receive $10 (positive incentive). In other words, losses loom larger than gains, so use negative, rather than positive, external incentives to get your way[109].

---

[108] Lo, Andrew W., Dmitry V. Repin, and Brett N. Steenbarger. *Fear and greed in financial markets: A clinical study of day-traders*. No. w11243. National Bureau of Economic Research, 2005.

[109] Tversky, Amos, and Daniel Kahneman. "Loss aversion in riskless choice: A reference-dependent model." *The quarterly journal of economics* (1991): 1039-1061.

- *Example: Focus on negative incentives rather than positive ones.* For example, imagine that you are remorselessly pestering and a tightfisted business partner to give you a lucrative contract. We know that fear usually trumps greed, so hit the guy with negative external incentives rather than positive external ones. Don't concentrate on the doubtless *benefits* of working with you (the value of your incredible expertise and experience). Instead concentrate on the terrible *costs* of *not* collaborating (the apocalyptic risks to his business and lifestyle if he misses out on the incredible value you can add).

- *Example: Frame incentives as negative rather than positive.* For example, do not grandiosely brag to your target that "If you invest in this business, you could *make* up to $100,000 per year." Instead warn forebodingly that "If you *don't* invest in this business, you might *lose out* to the tune of $100,000 per year." The content of what you are saying is exactly the same in both cases, but you are framing your message more effectively with the latter phrasing.

WE FOCUS ON THE PRESENT AT THE EXPENSE OF THE FUTURE

The timing of external incentives is also vital. It is a natural human tendency to live for today and leave tomorrow to look after its damn self. So individuals respond like slobbering dogs to immediate incentives while paying little heed to those things which will occur in the more distant future. This is even the case if the immediate incentives are considerably smaller[110].

In terms of positive incentives, for example, most will prefer one glass of quaffable champagne today to two glasses tomorrow. Indeed, they often prefer one glass of champagne today to a generously large bottle of the stuff in a decade's time.

People react to nasty things (negative incentives) in a similar fashion. Imagine you are scheduled for a highly unpleasant appointment at the dreaded dentist's office in five years' time. This disagreeable storm cloud is so far away on the horizon, it occurs so far in the future, that you can effectively forget about it. However, if you were booked-in for that same dental procedure

---

[110] Benzion, Uri, Amnon Rapoport, and Joseph Yagil. "Discount rates inferred from decisions: An experimental study." *Management science* 35, no. 3 (1989): 270-284.

at 9:00 a.m. the next morning, then the thought of it would loom over you threateningly, like a menacing thunderstorm.

Expert persuasion professionals know that it is possible to deviously exploit this psychological phenomenon to control the behavior of the unsuspecting "man in the street." They do this through cleverly manipulating the timing of incentives, bringing them forward in time to make them more effective or pushing them back to make them less so. In terms of timing, *today* has a particularly magical power. People love receiving positive incentives *today* and hate incurring negative incentives *today*.

The fact that folks often take such a shortsighted view of the vital business of attaining pleasure and avoiding pain explains a wide range of strange human behavior, which otherwise seems incomprehensibly foolish.

Take the foul habit of smoking as an illustration. There are numerous ghastly health-related negative external incentives associated with smoking (i.e., heart disease and lung cancer). However, hardened nicotine addicts pay these horrible diseases scant regard. This is because they often don't occur until decades later. They think, *I know that smokers die from cancer in their sixties, but to hell with it. I am only forty. I will cross that bridge when I come to it.*

Moreover, the guilty pleasure from smoking is gratifyingly instant—you experience the smooth nicotine buzz as soon as you spark up a ciggy and inhale. This immediate chemical stimulus makes you perceive the positive incentives (including the benefits of avoiding nicotine withdrawal) as all-important.

Since smokers experience the subjective positive incentives of smoking as large (because they are immediate) and the negative incentives as small (because they are distant), they continue to puff away[111]. Unfortunately the long-term effect of their choices is an earlier and nastier date with the Grim Reaper.

- *Example: To incentivize your target to purchase your products and services, make positive external incentives immediate and delay negative external incentives.* For example, in terms of making positive incentives immediate, offer "same-day delivery" or "cash back" offers. In terms of delaying negative incentives, you could introduce "buy now, pay later" deals or facilitate the target to use your business's own in-house line of credit, or a major credit card, to push back the pain of parting with their hard-earned cash.

- *Example: Persuade your target to agree to a favor by praising them immediately for helping you but asking them to perform the favor at a much later date.* For example, imagine that you want a coworker to spend a

---

[111] Thaler, Richard H. "'Some Empirical Evidence on Dynamic Inconsistency." *Quasi rational economics* 1 (1991): 127-136.

few weeks of their time helping you renovate an investment property. Put yourself in their shoes. They face a positive internal incentive in terms of the psychological satisfaction associated with helping a friend in need (because a friend in need is a friend indeed!). However, they also face a negative internal incentive in taking time out of their hectic schedule to lend their lazy old buddy a hand. To persuade them, they must see the positive incentives as outweighing the negative, and issues of timing are crucial to this.

- The positive internal incentive of helping a friend is *immediate*, so, psychologically speaking, it packs a powerful punch. However, the negative internal incentive of sacrificing their time seems like small potatoes because it is *so far away*. Therefore, manipulating the timing of things will help you get your wicked way.

- By the same token, if you want to persuade a target *to not do something*, then emphasize that the costs will wallop them imminently, but they wouldn't receive a smidgen of benefit until some far away point in the dim and distant future.

CHAPTER SUMMARY

In Chapter Three, I explained how to expertly wield eight persuasion weapons to revolutionize your outer game:

- Using prime wording to control your unsuspecting target on a subconscious level

- Dazzling your target with smoking-hot looks

- Looking like a big shot to leverage the psychological power of authority

- Making friends in order to influence people

- Employing hypnotic language patterns to bypass the gatekeeper and directly access the subconscious mind

- Proving popularity so the sheep will follow

- Obligating using nifty commitment devices

- Nudging cleverly using incentives

Congratulations, agent! You have completed your training. You are now ready to commence your daring mission to join the hallowed ranks of the superrich. Please read on to find out how to register for your free webinar.

EPILOGUE: GO OUT AND

CHANGE THE WORLD

As your secret agent success training draws to an end, hopefully you are bursting with a tremendous sense of excitement about the magical future that will now open its doors to you. The wisdom you have learned, if you effectively apply it, can allow you to do *whatever* you want, *whenever* you want, *however* you want, with *whomever* you want. Now get into the real world and put it into action.

By now you might also have discovered the hidden esoteric secret, which is peppered throughout the pages of this book. If so, then congratulations! If not, then don't worry. Reread the book and reflect more deeply on its message.

So let the adventures begin, and good luck with your mission to join the ranks of the superrich. And remember, "If there is a will, there is always a way my friend"[112]

---

112 Quote by Richard Kuklinski- The Iceman.

SIGN UP FOR YOUR FREE WEBINAR AND
BRAINWAVE ENTRAINMENT AUDIO FILE

If you haven't done so already, then act now to secure your place on my free $299 webinar by emailing **secretagentmethod@gmail.com** with "Send me my free gifts" in the subject header, and with a scanned copy of the sales receipt from your purchase of this book as an attachment. This unique experience imparts powerful information on how to tailor your inner game training to suit your own personality's strengths and weaknesses, and how to access an elite network of Secret Agent Method practitioners. We will also send you your free brainwave entrainment files in response to the same email.

APPENDIX: SIX WAYS TO MAKE THIS BOOK HIGHLY EFFECTIVE IN MAKING YOU RIDICULOUSLY RICH

- Don't just give this book a cursory skim read and then forget about it. You will gain the most benefit from treating it as your own personal manual on how to become a billionaire. Whenever you have a spare five minutes, whether it's on the train or relaxing at home, flick through it and reflect on the wisdom in these pages.

- Faithfully follow the instructions in this book like a devout puritan would his holy text. Don't imagine that you are smarter than the book and pick and choose which bits to apply. The advice I give is part of a perfectly functioning and balanced system. If you remove one element of the system, the whole thing breaks down, and you will not become filthy rich.

- Do the exercises *in real life*. Practice is the magic key to success. Just like the karate grand master develops his expertise through constant repetition, you must keep honing and refining your skills. By performing the techniques, you will learn. As Bernard Shaw said, "If you teach a man anything, he will never learn." It's all about learning by doing rather than just by understanding theory.

- Set yourself stretching targets for effectively applying the techniques in this book. For example, say to yourself, "I will spend thirty minutes per day on brainwave entrainment," or "I will use primes eight times each week." Ask your friends and family to give you a small reward (e.g., money, your favorite food, or so on) every time you successfully hit your target.

- Each week set aside some quiet time (around half an hour would work well) to reflect on how skillfully you have applied the techniques and how you could take things to the next level of accomplishment.

- *Memorize* some of the key techniques to retain the core knowledge at your fingertips. Luckily memorizing things is a piece of cake, if you know the tricks. I don't have time to go into the details here, but you will find some clever stuff at *www.mindtools.com*.

www.ingramcontent.com/pod-product-compliance
Lightning Source LLC
Chambersburg PA
CBHW071212090426
42736CB00014B/2785